Collins first-time gardener

Collins

Collins
first-time
gardener

A step-by-step guide for the gardening novice

Kim Wilde

This paperback edition published in 2006

First published in 2006 by
Collins, an imprint of
HarperCollins Publishers
77–85 Fulham Palace Road
Hammersmith
London w6 8jb

The Collins website address is:
www.collins.co.uk

Collins is a registered trademark of HarperCollins Publishers Ltd

14	13	12	11	10	09	08
7	6	5	4	3	2	1

Text © 2006 Wildeflower Ltd
Editorial, pictures and design © 2006 HarperCollins Publishers Ltd
except for pictures credited on page 224.

Kim Wilde herby asserts her moral right to be identified as the author of
this work.

A catalogue record for this book is available from the British Library.

Project manager: Emma Callery
Photographer: Nikki English
Designer: Bob Vickers

For HarperCollins
Commissioning editors: Angela Newton and Jenny Heller
Editor: Alastair Laing
Designer: Wolfgang Homola
Senior production controller: Chris Gurney

978-0-00-727078-1

Colour reproduction by Colourscan, Singapore
Printed and bound by Imago, Singapore

Contents

Introduction

Gardening for me began as a therapy, a way to restore myself from a hectic schedule of travelling and performing. I vividly remember returning from a working trip abroad still dressed in tight black trousers and a shoulder-padded jacket and going straight out into the garden to train my pyracantha. I haven't changed much and still often garden in completely inappropriate clothing such as nightdresses and platform mules! Now, as a busy working parent, my garden has never been so essential and has most definitely saved my sanity on more than one occasion. In our increasingly stressful and busy lives, a place to relax and re-charge our batteries is more and more important; modern living often sets a pace that can wear people down. A leafy sanctuary provides the perfect antidote, somewhere that offers peace and tranquillity, a place to unwind and share quality time with family and friends.

Gardens are not only good for the spirit, but good for the environment too. Plants absorb atmospheric pollutants as they produce food for themselves to grow, a process called photosynthesis, which at the same time releases oxygen back into the atmosphere. Plants also encourage wildlife, whose natural habitats are increasingly under threat from modern living. The simple pleasure of seeing birds, squirrels and ladybirds in the garden must not be underestimated. While being close to nature has a positive impact on our mental health, our gardens can become havens for wildlife, providing them with food, water and shelter without making any compromises to a chosen garden design.

The educational value of gardening should not be underestimated either, and schools are increasingly incorporating it into their teaching, often by creating wildlife or sensory gardens. In fact, I strongly believe that gardening for children is a natural; I've never come across a child yet who wasn't completely entranced by a pot of garden soil! Encouraging them to appreciate their natural world is a greater gift than any bought in a toy shop. Research shows that gardening can no longer be treated as a trivial pursuit, but instead it can be used as a valuable tool in helping vulnerable adults overcome a wide range of health and social problems by boosting their self-esteem and confidence.

Gardening not only provides the feel-good factor, but is a wonderful way to exercise. Of course, by this I don't mean a gentle potter in and out of the shed. Like all moderate cardiovascular exercise, it can help lower blood pressure and even heart disease and strokes. Just being out in the sunshine helps the body to make vitamin D, which is essential for healthy bones.

First-time gardening

First of all decide what your level of commitment is. Do you have the budget and the energy for a whole garden makeover, or do you simply want to make the best of what you've got? Write down your garden wish list, not forgetting to include the more practical elements like where the shed or the washing line goes, but don't restrict your imagination.

Think, too, about how you would like to style your garden. For instance, if you live in the country, you could reflect the natural, rural surroundings by using timber fencing, old bricks and rustic arches, setting the perfect stage for roses, lavender and marigolds. Urban homes often suit garden styles that reflect the design and materials of the house, and perhaps the use of 'architectural' plants with strong place and presence; very small urban gardens may even reflect the styling from within the house.

I wanted my own garden to have a more formal design close to the house so I planted clipped box balls and used reclaimed York stone and granite setts for the hard landscaping. I also made a small formal herb garden close to the kitchen's back door (within easy grabbing distance from the plot to the pot!). Further away from the house, gravel paths meander and ornamental grasses and daisy-like flowers, such as echinacea, are planted informally, reflecting the natural style of the surrounding meadows. Ultimately, styling a garden is a very personal choice, but always take into account the location, the site and the style of the house.

Measure your garden and take time to experiment with different design ideas using simple shapes, remembering that strong design does not have to be complicated. Small gardens often suit a more formal design than an informal one, perhaps using simple shapes such as squares and circles. Setting a design at 45 degrees to the house is a tried and tested design option that encourages the eye to move from left to right, creating a space that feels much bigger than it actually is. Also think about incorporating a change in level to create interest; pergolas and arches to add height; potential seating areas to enjoy different parts of your garden; perhaps a simple water feature.

It may seem to the first-time gardener that there really is far too much to have to take into consideration, and this is exactly how I felt when I started. But don't be discouraged if the pieces of the puzzle don't fit together as quickly as you would like. The first steps of any pursuit are always the hardest – remember learning to drive?

I have loved writing this book and sincerely hope that anyone reading it will start their own personal journey into a magical and absorbing world. I have made many good friends along the way who have shared my love of plants and gardens and I dedicate this book to them.

Part 1
GARDENING BASICS

A garden can transform the quality of your life and that of your friends and family. We all have memories of gardens as children, perhaps an apple tree, Grandma's roses or the smell of freshly mown grass. Whether you have just a small window box or a larger garden space, you can discover the gardener in you, the gardener that I believe lives within us all. Creating your garden can be a very personal and exciting journey, and armed with some gardening basics we can all have our own personal Eden.

What makes a good garden?

We all have our own idea of what would be our perfect garden. I know that many times I have visited gardens and thought how wonderful they are. I often looked in awe at these lovely creations and thought how difficult it would be to design such a garden for myself. Remember, however, that beauty is in the eye of the beholder – garden design is entirely a personal matter. No two of us are exactly the same and it is in that difference that we find appreciation, enjoyment and pleasure. So whatever your particular aesthetic leaning, be confident to set out to achieve the look that pleases you. If it is right for you, then who can say it is wrong?

If you begin to look closely at what a garden is, how it has been constructed and also understand how it works, then creating your own great garden begins to become a real possibility. We can all learn a lot by visiting other gardens, and looking at how they are planned and arranged. We can then apply those principles to our own garden space. You will be surprised at what encouragement and inspiration you will pick up from other gardens. Don't just visit large, splendid gardens, many good ideas and inspirations can be had from just taking a stroll through your local neighbourhood. Not only is there the opportunity of picking up some good ideas, you will also begin to learn about which plants grow well in your particular area. Just as importantly, you will see those that struggle to survive and so you will be able to decide whether or not they will even be a part of your planting plan.

Books and magazines are also packed with inspiration. Magazines in particular are great for cutting out pictures of gardens, favourite plants and planting schemes that appeal to you, all of which can be kept. Why not start a seasonal profile, cutting out images of plants that look good at different times of the year, to help you plan for year-round colour? Details such as these are easily forgotten. Rosemary Verey's *Garden Plans* was the first gardening book I owned and was the inspiration for the initial layout of our garden. I knew little about gardening and garden design then and have since developed a more personal style of gardening, but it was a helpful starting point. We've all got to start somewhere, and as I often say, 'You don't have to be different to be good ... to be good is different enough.'

Nor does it matter if you only have a small garden: the principles of good layout and design still apply, whatever size space you have to work with.

This picture shows how good design doesn't have to be complicated. Here a rectangle and semi-circle form the basis for a stylish urban garden. The space has been divided into rooms with the use of trellis, which together with the planted containers, provides height and helps screen the seating area and lawn from each other.

Working with the landscape

Well-planned gardens use their available space efficiently, taking advantage of any natural features such as an eye-catching view. In an urban landscape this may be an attractive nearby building, a mature tree or a view of the cityscape. In a more rural setting, there may be an opportunity of a view across open countryside, perhaps to mountains, hills, a distant steeple or a faraway, isolated village.

Many garden designers call this 'borrowing the landscape' and this technique can be used to wonderful effect, often creating a visual illusion of extending the garden horizons. Look around your garden to see if this is an element that you can take advantage of in your own design. If there are no natural features that you can incorporate in your plan, it is perfectly possible for you to create beautiful vistas within the garden itself.

The continuous brick path and formal layout of the clipped box (Buxus) naturally lead the eye to the statuary beyond. It's a perfect focal point.

Focusing attention

In larger gardens, statues and sculptures are used on a grand scale to create focal points. However, simple features such as a specimen plant, birdbath, water feature or seat can also be used as very effective focal points, drawing the eye to them. In a smaller space, the use of a focal point can help make the area feel larger than it is.

I find that seats are a particularly good item to use in this way as they also offer an attractive invitation to sit and rest. Think carefully about where you place a seat. For instance, is there a place in the garden that gets the last spot of evening sun? This would be a good location for a seat. A seat also gives you an opportunity to think carefully about what you plant around it. I would suggest that night-scented plants should be considered. There is nothing more pleasant than to experience the concentrated scents from flowers and foliage in a sheltered spot in a garden, on a summer's evening, when the air is still and warm.

This small area has been turned into a garden room by using rusted iron containers and a matching archway, which successfully divide it from the main garden area and simultaneously create a wonderful entrance.

Creating different spaces

Garden designers will often make the best possible use of space in a garden by dividing it into several smaller units, or 'rooms'. This makes the space more interesting to the mind and to the eye: a garden that cannot be seen in one glance invites further exploration. You will want to wander round it, to visit all the rooms – and this is often why a visit to an average-size public garden can take so long! The clever layout means we walk over the same piece of ground, often crossing our tracks and also viewing the same features from different angles.

The division of the garden into rooms can be achieved in many ways. The planting of evergreen shrubs or hedging is an effective divider, providing year-round colour and maintaining an integrity of structure throughout the year. Or you might prefer a less permanent divider, such as trellis, which can offer you an easier means of changing the layout of the garden as your own ideas change and develop.

My outdoor dining room, where a vine-covered pergola provides shade from the midday sunshine.

Whichever way you choose to create the division of the garden, this design strategy can also serve some very good practical purposes. Utility areas can be screened out of sight and areas of shelter will also be created, which can be used to the benefit of both people and plants. Furthermore, a room design is a way of allowing you to choose either diversity in the garden, where each room is differently themed and planted accordingly, or indeed to choose continuity between rooms by implementing the planting of the same structural plants in each area. My garden has developed into a series of rooms from a shady courtyard to a sunny, late summer border. I have used various hedge solutions as well as trellis to help both divide the space and provide shelter.

Light and shade

Well-designed gardens also use light to best effect. The contrast between bright light and shade in a garden can have many different qualities. Shafts of sunlight falling into an otherwise shady area will transform a space, especially where these shafts light up a water feature. Too much light, however, can also be a problem. I am sure you know how welcome it is to seek the comfort of shade on a hot, sunny day. If shade is not a natural part of your garden, it can be created by the careful siting and planting of trees. Or use climbers, as in my garden, where a leafy vine-covered seating area provides pretty, dappled shade and so is the perfect area for relaxing and entertaining.

Evening light can be usefully employed, too. Planting trees or shrubs with coloured leaves in such a way that they are backlit by the setting sun can create a dramatic and pleasing effect at the end of the day. Ornamental grasses also look particularly beautiful when backlit. We have giant feather grass (*Stipa gigantea*) planted in a position where it casts a silhouette in the morning and is then bathed in warm sunlight by late afternoon. As the sun sets behind it, the seed head plumes look quite lovely.

Keeping things to scale

Correct scale in a garden is vital. For example, planting a large viburnum next to a delicate bellflower (*Campanula*) is not going to be a successful combination. On visiting a great garden it's easy to take scale for granted, but we would soon notice if it wasn't right. This applies in smaller spaces too: correct scale means features such as sculpture, pots, furniture and plants sit at ease within the garden and also with each other, working both individually and as a whole. An out-of-scale sculpture or feature will upset the overall balance of the garden.

Consider the relationship of all elements within the garden with regard to scale. Successful use of scale means all elements are in complete harmony and it will be imperceptible that you have carefully considered this aspect.

Limit the use of landscaping materials to achieve a sense of unity and allow the plants to do the talking.

Hard landscaping

The choice of hard landscaping materials is another important consideration that affects the feel of the garden. Patios, steps, timber decking and gravel areas are among many options available, but should be in proportion to the surroundings. Don't spend time, effort and money creating hard landscaping features when they are simply not required. An over-landscaped garden can look cold and soulless, lacking the essential balance between plants and man-made features. Where hard landscaping is required local natural materials, such as stone, brick or gravel, always sit more comfortably in a garden (see page 72). Never choose more than two or three materials as the overall look can quickly become restless and cluttered, and always refer your choices to your location, the site and the style of your house.

Aspect and light

The aspect of your garden plays a significant role in how your garden looks and feels, and to the kinds of plants that will flourish there. A garden with little shade that is baked by the summer sun may even be too hot to use in high summer, whereas shadier gardens will have a much cooler feel to them. In both these instances, the range of plants that you can choose is quite different. Plants that originated in the Mediterranean region such as lavender (*Lavandula*), rosemary (*Rosmarinus*) and lavender cotton (*Santolina*) will enjoy basking in the heat, and will have adapted through time to thrive in such conditions. Those plants with woodland origins such as ferns, snowdrops (*Galanthus*) and camellias are adapted to grow in shade and may suffer if planted in the same hot, sunny position. Many gardens have planting opportunities for both aspects, so make a note of where the sun shines in your garden throughout the day, and then make your plant choices accordingly.

In a sunny garden

In the northern hemisphere, gardens that have an open, south or westerly aspect are usually hot and sunny for most of the day. The way in which the sun falls in your garden is an important consideration in the planning of features, and as the sun sets in the west, this aspect

An open, sunny aspect is perfect for many perennials and shrubs.

*Here are some favourite sun-loving plants in my garden: French lavender (*Lavandula stoechas*), globe thistle (*Echinops sphaerocephalus *'Niveus'*) and the soft yellow* Phlomis russeliana.*

Small trees to provide light shade

Acer pseudoplatanus 'Brilliantissimum'
Amelanchier lamarckii (snowy mespilus)
Betula utilis var. *jacquemontii* (Himalayan birch)
Cercidyphyllum japonicum (Katsura tree)
Crataegus laevigata 'Paul's Scarlet' (May hawthorn)
Gleditsia triacanthos 'Sunburst' (honey locust)
Malus x *robusta* 'Red Sentinel' (crab apple)
Prunus x *subhirtella* 'Autumnalis' (Higan cherry)
Rhus typhina (velvet sumach)
Sorbus cashmiriana

KIM'S TIPS

> Use a compass to help you establish which direction your garden faces.
> For gardens in the southern hemisphere, all directions are reversed. So a south- or west-facing garden is predominantly shady, while a north- or east-facing garden enjoys plenty of sun.

will be bathed with warm evening sunshine – a great bonus for those of us that work during the daytime – and so is an obvious choice for an evening seating area. During high summer, a south-facing, warm, sunny wall may be uncomfortably hot, but during the colder months any warmth at all will be welcomed. In our open, south-facing garden, I especially enjoy my seat by the kitchen door, so that I can take pleasure in a little winter sunshine; perfect for enjoying morning coffee outside while I let the dog out!

If your garden is particularly hot and sunny due to its aspect, consider planting trees to create some light shade and shelter, or consider an arbour or pergola (see pages 98–103). Remember, too, that even in the hottest, driest spot, there are sun-loving plants that will flourish (see page 42).

In a shady garden

A northerly or easterly aspect will almost certainly mean more shade, but this doesn't mean it needs to be dark and dull. First, consider

thinning out some of the trees and tall shrubs to let in more light, and plant golden-leaved plants to lighten the shade, such as the golden-leaved mock orange (*Philadelphus coronarius* 'Aureus') or the golden-leaved dogwood (*Cornus alba* 'Aurea'). A plant with golden foliage will brighten any dark corner and many prefer to grow in part shade as full sun may scorch their leaves.

The shade cast by deciduous trees and shrubs will not come into full effect until the leaves appear. So if you underplant with spring-flowering bulbs, such as snowdrops (*Galanthus*), daffodils (*Narcissus*) and bluebells (*Hyacinthoides non-scripta*), they will complete their flowering season before the tree canopy closes up. Low light levels in shady gardens can make things appear to be smaller, so be bold with everything from layout (use generous paving areas) and ornament (choose large containers) to planting. Several exotic-looking bold architectural plants, such as the castor-oil fig (*Fatsia japonica*) and the Chusan palm (*Trachycarpus fortunei*), tolerate a little shade.

In shady courtyards, brightly painted walls will substantially increase light levels, while strategically placed mirrors will reflect more light into the space as well as making it appear larger than it is. Water, too, will reflect light, adding sparkle to shady corners while offering sympathetic planting opportunities for fabulous foliage associations, such as shade-tolerant ferns, foxgloves and arum. The larger blue-leaved hostas are easy to grow in such situations and are slug resistant too.

*Not all plants like full sun. Many ferns (**above**) are first and foremost woodland plants so, like foxgloves (*Digitalis*) and hostas (**right**), they are happy when growing in partial shade.*

Top bold shade-tolerant shrubs

Aucuba japonica (spotted laurel)
Camellia japonica (common camellia)
Fatsia japonica (Japanese aralia)
Hydrangea quercifolia (oak-leaved hydrangea)
Mahonia x *media* 'Charity'
Phormium tenax (New Zealand flax)
Prunus laurocerasus (cherry laurel)
Skimmia japonica
Trachycarpus fortunei (Chusan palm)
Viburnum davidii

Shelter

Shelter too is an important factor to take into account. Keeping out the wind increases the warmth of a garden significantly. Many plants can suffer from wind exposure (for example, they may have torn, tatty leaves), plus the soil dries out more quickly. Buildings, walls, fences and hedges all contribute to successfully reducing the exposure to wind. This, in turn, makes the garden a far more comfortable place for plants and people alike.

In windy situations, solid walls or fences may create turbulence on the sheltered side. To avoid this, use a slightly open fence, such as woven hazel, through which wind passes, but at a reduced speed. Hedges also allow for this filtering effect and can be a cheaper option than erecting fences or walls, while simultaneously providing colour and interest within the garden.

Formal hedges such as yew (*Taxus baccata*) may need clipping twice a year. Informal hedges such as laurustinus (*Viburnum tinus*) are generally left unclipped and are therefore more labour saving. Remember to plant evergreens – plants that do not shed their leaves – where privacy is of prime importance. Where security is an issue, plant tough, prickly hedges such as holly (*Ilex* x *altaclerensis* 'Golden King'), *Berberis darwinii*, firethorn (*Pyracantha* 'Mohave') and hawthorn (*Crataegus monogyna*), which all provide tough protection.

Hedges can add to the style of the garden, as well as providing structure and shelter.

Climate and weather

It is important to gain a broad understanding of your local climate. This will allow you to use it to your best advantage. To be forewarned is to be forearmed. Sometimes the weather can be the gardener's friend and sometimes it can be our foe.

If you gain a general understanding of your local climatic conditions in terms of its extremes, you can use this to influence the choice of plants in your garden. If you have cold and frosty winters, then it is no use expecting exotic plants to survive outside without protection. Alternatively, if you have long, hot summers, then there is not very much point in choosing plants that like to keep their roots wet.

Unfortunately, most of us only achieve a good understanding of our climate and its effect on our plants through trial and error. But a little bit of research and planning will increase your knowledge and save you valuable time, effort and money. There is a saying that, 'There is a plant for every condition.' Bear this in mind when choosing plants, not only for their specific positions, but also in terms of your prevailing climatic conditions. Do this and your garden will thrive. The most important climatic conditions to consider are temperature, wind, rainfall and humidity.

Even in cool temperate weather, microclimates within gardens can enable frost-sensitive plants such as tree ferns and Geranium maderense *to be grown.*

Temperature

There are two main aspects to consider – air temperature and soil temperature. Both of these are vital factors in determining the successful growth of plants. Almost all plants purchased from garden centres are now informatively labelled. There should be a maximum and minimum temperature given, between which the particular plant will do well. In some nurseries, stock is not always so well labelled, so don't be afraid to ask someone who works at the nursery if any

At present, this Agave americana *might not survive an average temperate winter. However, with milder winters due to climate change, such plants will become more commonly seen. In the right conditions, and over 30 years, these plants can grow up to 2m (6ft) high.*

plant you want to buy fits in to the maximum and minimum temperatures in your garden.

Frost is a hazard and can put plants at great risk. A frost occurs when the temperature falls below 0°C (32°F) on clear, still nights. Local weather stations measure the temperature 1.5m (2yd) above ground level, so if the forecast in your area is for a temperature of 4°C (39°F), the temperature of your plants at ground level could be close to freezing.

Severe frosts can damage or put at peril even hardy plants, but in general terms it is important to know when the danger of spring frosts is likely to be over in your area. It is only after this date that you should plant out tender plants and summer vegetables. If a frost is forecast, it is advisable that you protect any plants that you know to be at risk from such a low temperature (see pages 190–1).

You'll often hear the term 'frost pockets' used by gardeners. Frost pockets are low-lying areas such as valleys and hollows where cold air (which is heavier than warm air) flows downhill, accumulates and causes frost. So if you live in a valley or hollow you should take extra care against frost.

Climate change: Almost all scientists now agree that the earth's climate is changing. The effects of global warming are much debated and contentious, but there is widespread expert opinion agreeing that there will continue to be a general rise in temperature, with a resulting frequency of flooding and droughts, as well as other extreme weather conditions all over the world.

Global warming will deliver a mixed bag to us gardeners as milder winters will allow a greater number of tender species, such as citrus fruits, to be grown outdoors in temperate zones, as well as increased yields of many vegetables, fruit and flowers due to increasing levels of CO_2, which plants absorb in photosynthesis. Problems will include an increase in pests and diseases as well as increased maintenance to cover the longer growing season, and certainly many species of plants will suffer or face extinction. As gardeners we are all in a position to make a positive difference to our environment simply by planting and caring for plants appropriate to our environment. Recycling organic matter, improving the soil and planting for wildlife are just a few of the ways we can start to redress the balance and help to heal a planet that is under stress.

Plants you can expect to see more of include olive (*Olea europaea*), ginger lilies (*Hedychium*), banana (*Musa basjoo*), Canary Island date palm (*Phoenix canariensis*) and century plant (*Agave americana*).

Hedges are the perfect barrier for providing shelter from wind within a garden.

Wind

When it is severe or continuous, wind can cause much physical damage to plants. The best way to protect your garden from wind is to create windbreaks. These are simply plantings of trees or hedging that will reduce the speed of the wind by taking the brunt of the wind themselves, thus 'breaking' the wind. Natural windbreaks are generally more successful than man-made ones. So, if you have an area of garden that is particularly exposed to the wind, you should consider planting a screen of trees or shrubs that themselves are wind resistant. Ask advice from your local garden centre as to which plants these would be for your area.

Rainfall

Rainfall is an essential aspect of climate that provides the water for your plants to grow. In areas of low rainfall, irrigation schemes can be very effective, but even they still depend on rain falling at some time. Most of our gardens still receive the water that they need through regular rainfall. Unfortunately, rain does not fall at predictable intervals and in consistent quantities, so your plants need to be able to cope with this variability in rainfall. This can sometimes present two main problems:

Waterlogging of the soil, occurs with consistent heavy rain where drainage is poor.

Drought conditions, where rain is sparse over long periods and the soil has dried up and the ground has gone hard.

In both cases, action can be taken to improve matters. Drainage of waterlogged soil can be improved by the addition of coarse grit. Cultivation of the soil will further improve matters (see page 30). If the problem is persistent, a more complex solution has to be found, such as installing underground drains. This is an area where professional help should be sought.

In dry soil conditions, the addition of organic matter will assist water retention, but generally a regular watering regime has to be

Plants for wet positions

Betula nigra (river birch)
Caltha palustris (giant marsh marigold)
Gunnera manicata
Ligularia 'Gregynog Gold'
Lysichiton americanus (yellow skunk cabbage)
Matteuccia struthiopteris (ostrich fern)
Persicaria amplexicaulis (bistort)
Rheum palmatum 'Atrosanguineum' (Chinese rhubarb)
Rodgersia aesculifolia
Trollius europaeus (common European globeflower)

undertaken to ensure that the soil is kept moist. If you have free-draining soil and persistently dry conditions, then you should choose plants that suit the conditions. Grasses and many plants from the Mediterranean region are suitable for dry conditions. There is always an answer for whatever the situation.

Humidity

Humidity is the amount of water vapour in the atmosphere. It is also affected by the moisture content of the soil. At one extreme, high humidity can encourage the growth of mould and fungal diseases, while a low humidity can increase the rate at which plants dry out and wilt. Low humidity can be improved in a garden by introducing water features and soaking all hard areas and soil, occasionally hosing down with water. Gardeners often refer to this as 'damping down'. The opposite extreme to low humidity occurs mainly in rainforests, where plants adapt to these very particular conditions. Careful selection of moisture-loving plants is therefore important.

It is unlikely that you will have a perfect balance of all of these elements of climate in your garden, but a basic understanding of your local conditions will help enormously. Knowing that you can take some steps to work with the climate and not against it will help to improve your gardening results.

Below: Euphorbia myrsinites *naturally grows in exposed rocky places, and so is ideal for planting in a drystone wall.* **Below right:** Astilbes *are moisture-loving plants and are best grown in partial shade.*

Soil

Getting to grips with the stuff that you grow things in can save you a lot of wasted time and money. A plant adapted for boggy conditions will thrive in a heavy, clay soil with poor drainage. Planted in a well-drained, sandy soil, lavender will thrive just as it does in its native Mediterranean soil. Of course, you can contrive soil conditions by planting in containers or raised beds, but as it's usually not possible to change your type of soil, it is essential that you understand what you have.

You don't need a degree in chemistry to gain an understanding of the many different types of soil. Although you could spend many years learning about and specializing in soil types, the structure of the soil, the balance of nutrients in the soil and the constituent make-up of the soil, it just isn't necessary when you start out in your gardening endeavours. Instead, a simple appreciation of soil types and their respective strengths and weaknesses will do to get you started.

What is soil?

Soil is the growing medium for your plants. From soil, your plants will draw their water and their nutrients. The soil provides a base in which the plant is physically supported too. The fact that soil can do all of this shows you just what an amazing natural material it is.

Some people are lucky enough to have a good soil for gardening that needs little in the way of support and improvement. Others are less fortunate and have a soil that needs to be enhanced by improving the structure of the soil by adding organic material, such as manure, and improving the nutritional value of the soil through the addition of fertilizers (see pages 178–9). The types of soil that you may encounter are shown opposite.

Rhododendrons and azaleas both grow best in a soil that has a low pH value, which is usually referred to as 'acid soil'.

Soil types at a glance

TYPE OF SOIL	RECOGNIZING THE SOIL	PROS AND CONS	SOIL IMPROVEMENT
Clay soil	• Heavy, sticky soil that is difficult to work and dig. • If you take a handful and squeeze it in your fist, it will keep the shape that you have squeezed it in to.	• Often rich in nutrients and highly moisture retentive. • Often needs the addition of substantial amounts of grit, sand and organic matter to make it more workable and to help the drainage of the soil.	• Improving the soil (see page 30) will make it easier to work and easier for the plants to access the rich supply of nutrients from the clay.
Sandy soil	• The opposite of clay soil, it is a dry soil that is very free-draining. • A handful will flow freely through your fingers.	• Generally easy to dig and to work with. • Requires regular watering, although the soil's ability to retain water will be improved by organic matter. • Not as nutrient rich as clay soil.	• An annual autumn application of well-rotted manure or leaf mould as a top dressing, will greatly improve the structure of this type of soil. The application of fertilizer helps too.
Peaty soil	• Very rich in organic material and good at retaining moisture. • If you take a handful, it will be crumbly in texture, rich dark brown in colour and when squeezed will release some moisture.	• Very fertile but it can sometimes be too wet.	• Too much rain can make the surface soil bind together. Annual mulching can help prevent this happening.
Chalky soil	• A crumbly, shallow soil. • It is stony and very free draining.	• Has a reasonable supply of nutrients but it is usually alkaline, so not suitable for some acid-loving plants.	• Benefits from a regular addition of organic material to aid nutrient levels.
Silty soil	• Similar to sandy soil but a little more moisture retentive.	• Usually has a high level of nutrients, but it can dry out too much.	• Benefits greatly from the regular addition of organic matter to help prevent drying out.

Worms have been conditioning our planet's soil for millions of years by recycling organic matter.

Soil structure

Topsoil: This is the soil on the surface of your garden. It is the soil level that contains almost all of the organic matter that has been dug in to the soil or applied as a top dressing to the soil in autumn.

The topsoil is the most supportive and nutritious of the soil levels for your plants. It is from the topsoil that the plants will draw most of their moisture and nutrients. The depth of top soil will vary greatly from place to place. You are very lucky if you have two spade depths or more of top soil in your garden.

It is in the topsoil that almost all of the organisms and insects that live in the soil will be found. Many of these are beneficial to the soil. One of the gardener's best friends is the earthworm, which plays such an important part in the incorporation of organic material into the soil. Through all its wriggling around, it is a tireless worker in aerating the soil, improving the drainage and providing ideal conditions for encouraging root growth in plants.

Some new gardens have little or no topsoil at all, and if this is the case it will need importing into the garden. Topsoil is not cheap, but be aware that if you find yourself in this situation, it is crucial you don't stint on importing it. Any penny-pinching at this stage will come back to haunt you in the years to come! Existing topsoil can also be increased with the addition of generous quantities of organic matter (see page 30).

Subsoil: This is the level below the topsoil and it usually differs in colour from the topsoil. It is often lighter in colour. One reason for this is that none, or very little, of the applied organic material reaches down to this level. The subsoil will still contain nutrients from which your plants will benefit, but it will not be anywhere near as fertile as the topsoil.

If, when you are digging, you reach subsoil, stop! Do not incorporate subsoil into the topsoil. You will know you have reached subsoil not only with a change in colour, but also as this layer will be more densely packed than the topsoil. You will undoubtedly have worked hard to achieve your desired structure and quality of topsoil. It will not assist you to then integrate subsoil into this valuable mix.

The pH value of your soil

Depending on what you intend to plant in the garden, it may be useful for you to know the pH of the soil. Some soils are naturally acid, and

Testing your soil

If you wish or need to know the pH of your soil, you can buy a soil testing kit from your local gardening centre. They are simple and easy to use:

1. Mix a small amount of soil with a chemical solution in a test tube.
2. Shake the tube and the solution will change colour.
3. Match the resultant colour against a colour chart supplied in the kit. This will correspond to a pH value and tell you to what degree your soil is acid or alkaline. Neutral soil has a pH of 7; a lower number indicates an acidic soil and a higher number, an alkaline soil.

Below: Rhododendrons are not difficult to grow, but they do require an acid soil to do well. *Right:* Lavender originates from the rocky terrain of the Mediterranean and manages well in dry, stony soil.

some soils are naturally alkaline. There are plants that will only grow in an acid soil and, conversely, there are plants that will only grow in an alkaline soil. However, this is looking at both extremes of a soil's acidity or alkalinity. Local climate will give you a clue as to whether your soil is alkaline or acid. High rainfall areas often have acidic soils as the rain leaches out alkaline elements in the soil, whereas alkaline soils are typically found in low rainfall areas. Classic acid-loving plants include heather, camellia, rhododendron, pieris and hydrangea. Classic alkaline plants include lilac, clematis, wisteria, rosemary and ceanothus.

Soil can be tested to see how acid or alkaline it is. The test is known as a pH test. The pH value ranges on a scale of 1 to 14. A pH value of 1 is very acid and a pH value of 14 indicates that the soil is very alkaline. A value of 7 is regarded as neutral.

The best soil

It is generally accepted that a neutral to slightly acidic pH would be the most beneficial in order to grow the widest range of plants. So a pH value somewhere between 5 and 7 would be ideal.

Alkaline soils are a problem if you wish to grow rhododendrons and heathers as both of these species thrive in acidic soils. Alkaline soils are also problematic because of their high level of calcium. Calcium increases the rate of decomposition of organic material, making it necessary to add manure to the soil more often.

Improving and buying soil

The most important thing you can do to keep all the plants in your garden happy and healthy is to improve your garden soil. The best way to do this is to increase the amount of organic matter that it contains by adding your own garden compost or well-rotted farmyard or stable manure. This last needs to be at least a year old because fresh manure can actually kill plants.

Organic matter consists of the dead and decomposing remains of animal and plant life and gives better overall soil fertility. Among other things it provides nutrients for plants, improves drainage, and helps retain moisture in the soil. Garden compost, farm manure, leaf mould and spent mushroom compost, are just some of the more common sources of organic matter. Any of these are not only good for improving the soil, but they can be used as a mulch to conserve moisture and suppress weeds if spread generously across the surface of a bed. Over time, worms will incorporate the mulch into the soil below. Organic matter incorporated into clay soil in the autumn will open it out, allowing more freedom for the circulation of air and water, promoting healthy root growth. Digging organic matter into sandy soils in the autumn will improve water and nutrient retention by acting like a sponge. Incorporate it into the soil whenever possible. I also make good use of potting compost that has already been used for seasonal bedding plants, spreading it across the vegetable garden and lightly forking it in before sowing seeds.

If you are starting to tackle your garden for the first time, the more you can do to improve your soil before planting the better. I have seen newly planted shrubs in poor, unimproved soil that, after a couple of growing seasons, have hardly made any growth at all. In soil that has had plenty of organic matter to bulk it up, the same shrubs would be almost mature in the same time.

The soil in our garden was originally poor, dry and free draining; I have selected plants that are suitable for this type of soil but I also continually improve the soil.

It is hard work though! When you finally manage to persuade your local farmer or stable owner to deliver you a load of well-rotted manure you will suddenly realize that it's heavy, and it takes a lot of effort to move it all around the garden! But once the job is done, you can sit back, safe in the knowledge that the worms will get to work on it, pulling it down into the soil, and eventually the organic mulch will add nutrients and structure to the soil.

KIM'S TIPS

> Plants are only as good as the soil that they grow in, so develop a regular habit of making your own compost, and enriching your soil with it whenever possible.
> If well-rotted manure isn't available from a local farm, you can buy or order it at garden centres.

Incorporating organic matter into soil greatly benefits the whole garden, not just raised vegetable beds.

Buying topsoil

If you are redesigning your garden, or if your existing soil is very poor, you may decide that you need to bring in some extra topsoil. The quality of topsoil for sale can vary a lot, so it's always best to look at it before buying it. Ideally the soil should be dark – humus rich – crumbly and free from stones and perennial weeds. Also get some advice on how much you need for any particular space – a couple of tonnes may sound a lot, but when it is spread out it doesn't go that far.

- If you need a lot of soil to increase ground levels in a garden area, an average quality of soil will be okay. You can then incorporate organic matter into the top layer to improve the quality further.

- If you just need a small amount of topsoil for a planting layer over existing poorer soil, it's really best to buy a more expensive 'screened' grade of soil. Screened soil has been sieved to remove stones and also any rubbish and most weeds.

It is also worth contacting your local council as many of them now operate a composting scheme where garden waste, cardboard and other biodegradable materials are collected from designated household bins and are composted on a massive scale. The resulting compost produced from these recycled materials makes an excellent soil conditioner and can save the need for buying large quantities of topsoil – and help the environment at the same time.

Basic botany

Plants play the most important role in the cycle of life on our planet. Without plants, there would be no human or animal life on Earth. It is believed that millions of years ago, algae that grew in the planet's seas somehow triggered the evolution of land living plants. These then in turn provided food for land-living animals as they evolved.

Mosses and conifers were some of the earliest plants and so didn't reproduce through flowers.

The oxygen we breathe also comes from plants as a byproduct of photosynthesis, which is the way a plant makes food for itself, and as part of this process plants also produce oxygen.

Leaves are the main food-making part of most plants. Chlorophyll is the green part of the leaves and captures energy from the sun. Using carbon dioxide and water, the leaves produce food in the form of sugars and starches, which provide the plant with energy to grow. Plants take in the carbon dioxide through tiny holes in their leaves, just like the pores in our skin, and oxygen is released as a by-product of photosynthesis through these tiny holes.

The plants also take in the water they need through their roots and lose water again through the tiny holes in their leaves. This process of taking in water and releasing it again is called transpiration.

For millions of years, the plants that existed on our planet were very simple in form and did not even produce what we think of as seeds. These early plants included tree ferns, horsetails, mosses and some conifers. They produced spores to reproduce, rather than flowers and seeds. Indeed, we still refer to them today as 'non-flowering plants'.

Evolution eventually produced flowering plants that could spread themselves over greater distances by the dispersal of seeds. Through evolution, plants adapted to

Evolution has created plants with specialist features such as hairs to protect the leaves from extremes of heat. Some plants, such as cactus, have developed fleshy leaves to store water during periods of drought.

individual conditions, and it is estimated there are now over 260,000 species of plants identified.

There is now an incredible variety within the plant kingdom, from plants such as tiny alpines to the world's tallest living tree, a 'coast redwood' tree in California, which is over 112m (367ft) tall. The climate of different world regions also determines what types of plants can flourish there. Plants have adapted themselves gradually to enormous differences of climate and growing conditions throughout the world. It is not enough to just survive in some extreme conditions: plants need to flourish and propagate themselves too.

In regions of very low rainfall, plants like the cactus have developed water-storing tissue in their leaves and stems. Mediterranean plants have adapted to their environment by developing hairy or furry and also narrow or silvery leaves to protect themselves from extreme heat and drying winds and also to reduce transpiration as much as possible. Garden plants such as rock rose (*Cistus*), rosemary (*Rosmarinus*), lavender (*Lavandula*) and sage (*Salvia*) all come from this region, so they are perfect plants for a hot, exposed area in the garden. For shady, damp conditions, look for large, dark green leaves, such as hostas, which have adapted to maximize the amount of light that is received.

The opium poppy, Papaver somniferum *produces seeds that result in many self-sown seedlings.*

Pollination and seed production

Although plants have developed many ingenious ways of reproducing themselves, the most common is through cross pollination. This is where pollen from one plant is transferred to another to fertilize it. Most plants have flowers with the male and female parts present in each flower. However, they still need to be cross-pollinated with another flower. Many plants rely on insects, such as bees or butterflies, to transfer the pollen from one flower to another. Pollen is a useful source of protein for some insects, such as bees.

Insects are attracted to the flower by scent, colour and nectar. They are not deliberately pollinating flowers, but they are usually feeding on sugary liquid nectar produced by the flowers when the pollen is rubbed off the body of the insect. They carry pollen from flower to flower, while collecting nectar and pollen for themselves. After pollination, the plant produces a seed, which mostly grows protected inside the plant.

It's not always insects that pollinate the flowers. Plants may use the wind, birds or even bats as pollinators. With wind-pollinated plants – such as grasses, cereals and some trees – the flowers are very simple, with no bright colours or pleasant scent as they don't need to attract the insects. These plants have both male and female reproductive parts and they make a lot of pollen.

Low-allergen plants

Alchemilla mollis (lady's mantle)
Amelanchier lamarckii (snowy mespilus)
Anemone x *hybrida* 'Honorine Jobert' (Japanese anemone)
Cistus x *hybridus*
Cotinus coggygria (smoke bush)
Forsythia x *intermedia*
Hydrangea anomola subsp. *petiolaris* (climbing hydrangea)
Prunus x *subhirtella* (Higan cherry)
Stachys byzantina (lamb's ears)

KIM'S TIPS

> There are 10 million people in Britain who suffer from hay fever or have asthma, both of which are triggered off mostly by pollen. This can occur in spring, summer or autumn and makes the lives of sufferers unbearable.
> Grass pollen is one of the main culprits, so if you suffer, you should definitely think of eliminating lawns and replacing them with hard landscaping such as bricks, setts, gravel and decking as well as planting a selection of low-allergen plants.
> Many hedges too can produce pollen and should be replaced with low-allergen climbers or shrubs (see left).

Latin names

It can be very confusing when you first go to your local garden centre and are faced with long, difficult to pronounce Latin botanical names. However, they are used for good reason. Botanical Latin is like an international language used worldwide by botanists and plant enthusiasts. The method of naming was standardized by an eighteenth-century plant collector called Linnaeus.

While one plant may have several common names, it will only ever have one Latin name, which will also be the same worldwide. It helps if you can get to grips with some Latin names, as it avoids confusion when buying plants, or finding out more about particular plants.

The olive tree, Olea europaea. *Quite often the species name refers to where the plant has originated. In the case of the olive tree, it's clearly Europe.*

Understanding Latin plant names

All plants are classified into family groups, which have:

- **Family name,** referred to as genus (or genera if plural), the Latin word for 'family'.
- **Species name:** Within a family group of plants there will be differences in the plants, and these are the different species. This is the second part of a botanical name and it is called the specific name.

So, if I was a plant, my name would be *Wilde kim*! The first part of my name indicating my family, and the second part me as an individual.

So the olive tree is *Olea europaea*. *Olea* is the family name, or genus, and *europaea* the specific or species name. Sometimes a slight difference is discovered within a species and it is given an extra name to denote this. For instance, a variety of olive tree that had larger fruits and smaller stones was named 'El Greco', so its full botanical name is *Olea europaea* 'El Greco'. It is normal for Latin names to be written in italics, and any 'extra names' to be put into single quotation marks at the end.

Part 2
PLANNING YOUR GARDEN

When I first started gardening I remember feeling totally overwhelmed with the whole subject, yet at the same time I thought that slowly but surely it would start to make sense if I just had a go. I've since realized that although a positive approach is always the best one – after all, gardening is an intrinsically optimistic pursuit – you do have to have a plan. A good, well-researched approach will help you to create a garden that reflects your requirements and tastes, and you'll soon discover, as I did, that planning a garden is as exciting as making one.

Assessing your requirements

At first, the thought of tackling your garden properly may seem a daunting task, but this is where careful and considered planning comes in. Rather than rushing to sort out a small area of garden, and then deciding which bit to do next, it is much better to make one overall plan for the whole garden. After making a complete garden plan you can then gradually work through elements of it in your own time, and in a methodical way. This approach will also allow you to implement your garden design in separate stages. Not least, it will allow you to implement each stage as your budget allows. You can then plan for the expenditure required and fit your garden projects to your budget. Even if you only have a small budget available, there are still changes and improvements that you can make to any space.

Enhance what you already have

First, have a good look at your garden and decide what works, what you like that is already there and what you may be unhappy with.

Overgrown areas: Depending on the variety, many overgrown trees or shrubs may be partially cut back and rejuvenated, retaining some height, maturity and privacy. Quite often wall shrubs and climbers may get out of control and fall out from the wall; cutting them back and tying them in is the answer here (see pages 182–5). Large shrubs may have sprawled across a lawn and need removing or cutting back, too, and large trees could have their lower branches removed to allow more light and air into the garden; this is one job for a qualified expert.

Hard landscaping: As hard landscaping is expensive, it's worth looking at any existing paving to see if it could be retained. Old paving slabs may be pressure washed to make them look like new again, re-pointing can make a great difference, too. Paved areas could also have their shape changed by removing some slabs (for instance, taking out the corner slabs from a square or rectangular shape), perhaps replacing them with plants. Scrape away old, dirty gravel and replace it with new. If you have a large expanse of gravel or chippings, try planting evergreen shrubs or grasses to break up the expanse.

Old fences: Old fences can sometimes be repaired, saving further expense, although old fence panels are best replaced. Fence panels are often made from poor quality, thin timber strips and just don't last that long. Carefully remove them leaving the posts, which, if still stable, can

If you have a border that contains some mature shrubs, they can be cut back and rejuvenated if you want to keep them. It wouldn't take long to get these shrubs back into shape, giving a much more coherent feel to the whole aspect.

carry a new closeboard style fence. Closeboard, or featheredge fencing, outlasts fence panels by years and creates a fence that I find more attractive, more robust and secure, and much easier to maintain than panels. A closeboard fence is also easy and simple to construct even if you only have basic DIY skills (see pages 78–9).

Developing your ideas

If you have a generous budget to spend, you may wish at this stage to consider employing some professional help and advice. A good garden designer will be able to plan your garden to fit your needs, and money spent on this initially may save you making an expensive mistake in the future. Try to get a recommendation for a good garden designer from a friend or neighbour. Word of mouth based on personal experience is so much more useful than simply picking a business card pinned to the garden centre noticeboard.

Costs can be minimized if you wish to engage the garden designer for an advisory visit only. But always be sure that you ask for an explanation of costs and that you know what to expect from any visit that may occur afterwards.

Choosing a garden style

Just as your own home will have a style of interior decoration, so your garden should have a particular style too. The look of a garden is partly influenced by where you live and the range of plants that will flourish in your climate. In England, a cottage garden style is very popular, whereas in Northern Australia obviously a tropical garden is more appropriate – but that's not to say you can't create a 'tropical' garden in a temperate climate or achieve a cottage garden style in Australia.

Traditionally, houses and their gardens only used local materials, so gardens matched their houses and tended to sit comfortably within their locality. Nowadays, though, there are many strong influences both from other countries and from modern garden designers. At the same time, the range of plants that are available to buy has dramatically increased and construction materials have become more affordable and much more widely available.

Whatever style of garden appeals to you, decide whether you would like to have a complete garden in that style, or just a part of it. If you use the design principal of 'rooms' in your garden, you could choose to include a few different styles. A Mediterranean style area, for example, would need to be in the hottest, driest and sunniest part of your garden, while you could have a tropical-style border in a sheltered spot, close to a patio or decking area. A wild area would be best situated at the bottom of your garden, as far away from the house as possible.

Whatever your preference of garden style, like the inside of your house, the biggest influence on its character will be you. Be guided by the different approaches and design principles that are shown here and in other books and magazines, and don't worry about making the odd mistake – even the most confident gardener does that.

Cottage garden

Even though modern gardens with shiny metal, glass and plastic have become features of many garden shows, the traditional cottage garden style is still very popular. It is certainly the most romantic, and also the most comfortable style to live with. The main element of this traditional style is its informal plantings, mixing together masses of perennials, especially spires of delphiniums, hollyhocks and verbascum together with annual flowers such as lavatera, sweet peas and marigolds and climbers like honeysuckle and jasmine and, of course, deliciously scented roses. Old clay pots and traditional garden furniture add to the charm of this style.

Tropical garden

Possibly the furthest away from the cottage garden is a tropical style garden. Even in a climate not especially associated with heat, a tropical style is surprisingly easy to achieve. However, it looks best in an urban situation and works very well with modern furniture and accessories. Tender plants such as bananas and cannas will require some extra care to overwinter them, but it is well worth the effort.

The big impact for the tropical style comes from dramatic foliage. Large-leaved plants such as fatsia and paulownia work well with more architectural plants such as palms, bamboos and New Zealand flax. For flowers, fuchsias work really well, especially *Fuchsia magellanica*.

Plants for a tropical-style garden

Abutilon x *hybridum* (flowering maple)
Arundinaria (bamboo)
Brugmansia x *candida* (angel's trumpet)
Canna (Indian shot plant)
Eriobotrya japonica (loquat)
Fatsia japonica (Japanese aralia)
Fuchsia magellanica
Paulownia tomentosa (Chinese foxglove tree)
Phormium (New Zealand flax)
Trachycarpus fortunei (Chusan palm)

Opposite: Blue Aquilegia *'Hensol Harebell', double flowered buttercups (*Ranunculus acris *'Flore Pleno') and the soft pink flowers of* Pimpinella major *'Rosea' combine to evoke that romantic, cottage garden look.*

Right: Even in a cool climate, a summer planting of tender plants creates a tropical effect. A variegated brugmansia and purple-leaved cannas provide both attractive foliage and flowers – but they will need winter protection from frosts.

Mediterranean garden

Plants for a Mediterranean-style garden

Cistus spp. (rock rose)
Cordyline australis (cabbage palm)
Cupressus sempervirens (Italian cypress)
Lavandula stoechas (lavender)
Olea europaea (olive)
Pelargonium spp.
Phlomis fruticosa (Jerusalem sage)
Rosmarinus (rosemary)
Santolina virens (cotton lavender)
Vitis vinifera (grape vine)

Even if you don't live in the Mediterranean, many plants suited to that environment are surprisingly easy to grow, which means it is quite possible to plant a Mediterranean-style garden – just as long as you have plenty of that essential ingredient, sunshine. Despite being sun-loving and tolerant of dry conditions, many Mediterranean plants are also frost hardy, although they do need a well-drained soil to keep their roots dry in winter. Terracotta pots work well as containers and plants such as olives and citrus trees add that authentic touch. Using grit as a mulch around plants also looks very effective. Look for plants with bright colours, which are evocative of the Mediterranean, and many plants from that region also have aromatic foliage.

Gravel also forms an excellent backdrop for a Mediterranean-style garden. The first gravel garden I ever saw was at Beth Chatto's now legendary garden in Essex and I was quite overwhelmed. I could not believe how many beautiful plants were thriving in such seemingly inhospitable conditions. If you are thinking about converting a lawn into a gravel garden, you will first have to remove existing turf and eradicate perennial weeds. If you have a large area, hire a turf cutter to save time and your back. Turf weighs a ton! (Don't waste any turf – once removed, pieces can be stacked upside down and covered with black polythene for 12 months. This will rot down and make a crumbly, even textured loam suitable as topsoil.)

The area will need digging over, and if the soil is not already sandy or gravely, you will need to add plenty of grit or gravel as well as some well-rotted organic matter. You may consider hiring a Rotovator for this equally back-breaking task, but any investment made now will bring great rewards to your garden for years to come. Remember that plants from the Mediterranean region need full sun and dry roots in winter. Also, they look much better if they are spaced further apart than most plants.

Excellent drainage and full sun is essential for these succulents. Aeonium arboreum, *opuntia and aloe add that Mediterranean feel to any planting.*

Formal garden

Choosing between a formal or informal style is like deciding whether to wear jeans and T-shirt or a tweed suit. Most of us like a bit of both, although not at the same time, which is why it is wise to choose a style appropriate to the occasion and stick with it. Of course, in many gardens there is the opportunity to try out several styles, but the smaller the space, the better it is to use just one.

Formal designs work really well in small spaces and can help them appear bigger than they actually are. Furthermore, the formal style can take on quite different characteristics. For example, a formal Japanese-style garden would focus more on glorifying nature and use more natural lines as well as asymmetry. Conversely, formal gardens in the West usually reflect man dominating his landscape by using symmetry, geometry and proportion with a greater emphasis on hard landscaping details, and it is these things that essentially characterize the formal style. The use of focal points such as pots, sculptures or topiary is also associated with a formal setting.

The use of symmetry and focal points creates a strong feeling of formality in this garden, even though the planting style in the rest of the area is more relaxed and flowing.

Wild garden

Many people are now increasingly aware of wildlife and wish to attract birds, bees and butterflies into their gardens (see pages 156–8). Whenever you create a garden area they will all come, but to attract the greatest variety of wildlife, think of adopting a wild garden style, possibly just in one area, rather than for your whole garden.

If you have the space, grass that is left unmown is a wonderful feature. Mow a pathway through the long grass, and then you can explore the many wild flowers that appear in the long grass. These will, in turn, attract many butterflies, moths and other creatures. Plant native trees and shrubs, too, and also make use of cultivated varieties of native plants. Honeysuckles can be grown up any new or existing trees that you may have and they will attract moths, which will, in turn, attract bats.

Introducing water is possibly the single biggest thing you can do to attract more wildlife to your garden. An informal pond with plenty of native marginal plants (see page 91) will quickly attract frogs, toads and many invertebrates. A wildlife garden, then, is more of a feature than a garden style, but it does have a particular look, and can still be a very colourful affair.

Grass left unmown allows wild flowers to grow. Here ox-eye daisies (Leucanthemum vulgare) look delightful among the long grasses, and will encourage wildlife, too.

Contemporary garden

A favourite style for smaller urban spaces, where there may be no strong feeling coming from historic architecture or countryside views, a contemporary style usually relies on a degree of formality, often using strong geometric lines and plants with architectural qualities. Hard landscaping materials are usually sleek and modern, with stainless steel, glass, plastic and industrial metalwork being popular. A clean, uncluttered look is essential for creating a contemporary style of garden; smooth rendered walls are more effective than brick or stone; and because foliage often works better than flowers in this type of setting, masonry can be painted to be the main source of colour in the garden. Containers and furniture must also reflect the fashion of the garden. When selecting plants choose simple blocks or lines of single varieties; grasses, bamboos and evergreen shrubs work especially well with modern materials.

Plants for a contemporary garden

Buxus sempervirens (common box) clipped into geometric shapes
Calamagrostis x *acutiflora* 'Karl Foerster' (feather reed grass)
Carex buchananii (leatherleaf sedge)
Equisetum ramosissimum var. *japonicum*
Euphorbia mellifera (honey spurge)
Fatsia japonica (Japanese aralia)
Festuca glauca (blue fescue)
Miscanthus sinensis
Phyllostachys nigra (black bamboo)
Pittosporum tobira (Japanese mock orange)

The use of modern materials and carefully positioned sculpture all help to create a clean, crisp contemporary feel to this garden.

Drawing and developing a plan

If you decide not to get any extra help, the best thing to do next is to make a simple plan of your garden. It sounds boring, but without a plan you'll find it difficult to imagine what will easily fit into your garden space and the best way to arrange your garden. Don't worry if you think you cannot draw, you don't need to artistically gifted to sketch out a simple plan, and that's all we are doing here.

Follow the steps opposite so you can achieve an outline of your garden from which you will then develop your design ideas. You will need to take measurements of your garden first. If you do not have a long enough tape measure, use lengths of string have measured and cut to a set length (for instance, a 5m (5yd) and 10m (10yd) length). Tie the lengths of string to a cane at each end, stretch them out, and measure the remaining distance with your tape measure. Add the two measurements together to get your total distance.

When you have completed your scaled garden plan, scan or photocopy it so that you have new copies to hand on which to sketch out different ideas. Tracing paper could also be used.

The plan drawn on the opposite page shows a scale drawing of this contemporary urban garden. The design is set at 45 degrees to the house and has been based on the angles suggested on a 1m (1yd) grid. The triangular beds play host to a water feature as well as architectural planting, and the eye is led through the garden to a sunny, west-facing arbour at the end.

How to draw up a plan

1
Draw the outline of your garden on a piece of paper using a pencil so you can rub out mistakes, should you make them. Don't worry if it's not perfect. If the garden is a simple rectangular shape, that's easy. If it's a more complicated shape, try to indicate any changes to its width or depth.

2
Add any existing structures in the garden that you think you will ultimately be keeping, such as a mature tree or shrub, or a garden shed. At this stage, the outlines need only be approximate in their dimensions.

3
Indicate where north lies on the plan so that you can see where the sun rises and sets. This will help you to decide, for example, where a sunny seating area or a shady border could be situated.

4
Add measurements for the outer boundaries of the plot and also diagonal measurements, noting down each one on the plan as you go. For fixed features, measure how far these are from other points, such as the corners of the garden. This will then help you to place them accurately on your plan.

5
Redraw your plan on a fresh sheet of paper and to scale so that it is in proportion to the actual garden space. Use 2cm (1in) on your plan to represent 1m (1yd) in your garden, which represents a scale of 1:50 (1:36). Use a ruler to measure and draw your boundaries and transfer all your measurements to the plan. Draw over the pencil lines in dark ink and now you can start experimenting with your design.

6
When you are experimenting with different ideas, it can be very helpful to have an additional layer of tracing paper between your basic outline and your proposed plans. The grid on this additional layer shows 1m (1yd) squares, which helps you get a better idea of scale for any new additions you would like to add to the garden. You can either align the grid with the house or, as here, turn it through 45 degrees.

Developing your plan

Before going any further, get back in the garden, this time with your camera. Take photographs from different places and at different angles. Stand with your back against each of your downstairs windows too, as these photographs will highlight the view from inside your house. This is a very helpful adjunct to your ground plan. Sometimes a view from a living room or kitchen window can be important, especially in the colder months when you won't go outside into the garden so much. Photographs show you how your garden really looks. It's like having a fresh pair of eyes viewing it for the first time. You can also draw your ideas directly onto your photographs, or onto tracing paper placed over them.

It's also necessary to think about what you really want from your garden. So before you move onto thinking about what are the essentials of good garden design (pages 52–9), make a list of which features you feel are most important for your garden, as these can have a bearing on your layout. Use this list as a starting point for assessing your own requirements:

- A patio or decking area with table and chairs for relaxing and outdoor dining.
- A children's play area, possibly with their own patch of garden.
- Other seating areas in different parts of the garden.
- Lawned areas, formal or informal.
- A vegetable or herb garden.
- A garden shed, essential for storage of tools, bicycles, toys, etc.
- A barbecue area, close to your outdoor dining area.
- Water features.
- A pergola for shade, shelter and privacy.
- A greenhouse.
- New pathways, for practical or design purposes.
- New fences and hedges for privacy and shelter.
- A washing line.
- A place for the dustbins.
- A kennel for your dog.

Taking your outline garden plan, start to work through your list in conjunction with the ideas on the following pages, beginning with the most essential features. Decide on the best place for each feature, and roughly mark their positions either on one of your photocopied plans or on a tracing paper overlay.

*An outdoor dining area is number one on most people's requirements (**above**) ... and don't forget about the children either (**below**).*

How are you going to use the garden? Almost certainly you will want an outside dining space. Ideally this should be situated close to the house, within easy reach of the kitchen, to make it easier to dress the table and serve food. Dining *al fresco* is such an enjoyment and is something that you can take delight in at most times of the year. Make sure that this aspect is catered for in your overall garden design. Outdoor dining areas should be private too, so consider screening or the planting of some hedges if required. One clever way to provide more privacy is to erect a simple pergola across the top of the area, which would provide shelter from the sun and rain in addition to the extra privacy.

Do children need catering for? If so, they will need an area where they can play without worry of damage to plants. Any play area should be within close supervision from the house so you can keep an eye on the children and be immediately able to attend to their needs. There are many ways to encourage children to get more involved in the garden, and for them to have their own little patch to grow flowers and vegetables on is a great idea, even if it is only in containers.

A second seating area? If you have the room, a second seating area in a different part of the garden can be very useful. In summer or winter, one area may have a more pleasant temperature than the other. Ask yourself where is the last part of the garden that you get the evening sun? It may be the perfect place for an outdoor dining area or at least it could be a position for a seat or a bench. You may also want to create a secluded place where you can sit and read or just enjoy a snooze on a sunny afternoon. Or you could plant a hedge that will provide a 2m (6ft) tall screen or use a part of the house, a dividing wall or the garden shed to provide a quiet enclosure. If your garden is small, perhaps use a central decking or patio area surrounded by plants.

Do you want a lawn? In a small garden ask yourself if you really need a lawn. In the summer it may need cutting twice a week, every week, there will be occasional weeds to deal with and, of course, a lawnmower to buy and maintain. If you are going to keep your lawn, remember that you can easily change its size to fit your new garden layout, making it larger or smaller, or a more interesting shape (see page 58). You might want to consider changing some of the lawn to hard landscaping or have a path through borders instead. Smooth, rounded corners are much easier to push the lawnmower around than sharp corners, making the lawn quicker to cut and generally easier to maintain. It's also possible to fill in any hollows or smooth out bumps in an existing lawn. In fact, even an existing lawn in a poor state of health can be completely rejuvenated, saving money on otherwise replacing it.

If you do decide to replace your lawn, or create a new one, I would recommend turfing it (see pages 174–5). Seed sown lawns are slow to establish and more weeds germinate, while the new grass seedlings are developing. The other brilliant thing with turf is that it is instant.

Lawns provide a soft surface that is ideal for relaxation or recreation. They do require some simple regular maintenance though (see pages 202–9).

Vegetable plot? Many people nowadays are interested in growing their own vegetables. We get much pleasure from our vegetable plot and nothing can beat having your own supply of home-grown vegetables and herbs. Even a small space can provide a few vegetables. A vegetable plot or raised beds need to go on your plan in a sheltered but open, sunny part of the garden and preferably somewhere the hose reaches!

Would you enjoy a water feature? Water features are really popular. There is nothing more relaxing than watching fish in an ornamental pool and listening to the gentle sound of trickling water. Water features do not necessarily need fish, however, and there are some very simple ready-made features in most garden centres that circulate water using a pump, providing an attractive feature and, of course, that all important sound. These types of features also pose no dangers to young children, as there is no pool of water. If there are no children about, then there are many opportunities to install water into your garden in the form of a pool, in a way that fits your particular garden style. (See also pages 88–93.)

*Top: Even a small area can supply you with plenty of fresh herbs and vegetables. **Above:** It is possible to have the sound of running water without a pool to maintain.*

Objects best left hidden away

Some essentials are not that attractive to look at, so it's best to decide where these are to go early on in your planning and work around them.

Dustbins: These are a particular eyesore and need to be tucked away somewhere out of sight but also not too far from the house door.

The garden shed: An essential for most gardens, providing storage for garden tools, the lawnmower, bicycles and a portable barbecue, and also overflow storage from the house. Sheds really need an all-weather pathway to them, preferably without any steps to negotiate. New sheds are often the strong colour of new timber and staining yours a very dark brown will help it to stand out less. Shrubs are useful for screening sheds from view, and if trellis is attached, climbers may be used to cover them too.

Washing lines: These fall into the same category as sheds, although they are, of course, best sited in a sunny position, close to the house. They may still be screened off from view using trellis and climbing plants, brushwood screening may be added too for an instant screening effect.

The essentials of good garden design

Now you've done the thinking, it's time to put pen to paper. Whatever space you have available (even the smallest back yard), with just a bit of careful thought, it is possible to design a garden that will provide you with pleasure and enjoyment.

> Balance is all about equilibrium and producing visual stability between all aspects of the garden, from design to planting. For instance, a tall pergola needs an equal mass to balance it, either another tall pergola or tree, or a horizontal feature that is as wide as the pergola is tall. In planting, a balance of evergreen and deciduous trees and shrubs, or small, medium and large-sized foliage, will be more pleasing to the eye.

It is worth taking time to experiment with basic shapes on your garden plan, making sure they have evolved from the house and are proportionate to it. At the same time, aim for a balanced composition that is pleasing to the eye. If it looks good on paper, the chances are it will look good in the garden, too.

As you have only drawn a simple plan, refer to the photographs you have taken or go into the garden to remind yourself of other important factors that need to be considered. Slopes (see pages 64–5), overhanging trees and existing trees and shrubs all need to be taken account of and, indeed, those you want to keep should already be on your plan.

As you decide on the layout of your new garden, you can start to add some more details. You may need to put up new fences or plant hedges for extra privacy, security or shelter. Shelter can affect the type of plants you can grow, and how well your plants do. It also affects your comfort in the garden (see page 21).

Of course, the plants are the stars of most people's gardens, but from a design point of view it's best to tackle the layout and arrangement of the garden first. On your plan, just be general to begin with, thinking about, for example, where you would like to see a mass of shrubs, climbers for screening, or suitable trees. Keep referring to your photographs, too – when you consider how you are going to arrange the layout of the garden, ask yourself how it will look from each window.

Get the balance right

A garden can be described in terms of masses (i.e. planting, sheds, pergolas) and voids (i.e. open spaces, such as patios or lawns). A well-designed garden is a balance between the two and too much void is a common design weakness: just think of the long garden with a wide lawn and narrow borders on either side.

To illustrate how masses and voids are best balanced, first draw a rectangle of about 30 x 20cm (12 x 8in) on paper to represent a garden, and then cut out circles, squares and rectangles of various sizes in card or stiff paper. The shapes represent the potential voids – patio, paths, lawn – in the garden. Arrange them to create different patterns within the rectangle. This is a really useful exercise and if you apply the principle to your own garden outline, it can be a particularly good way to get a design started.

Use the grid system

The main features in the garden, such as the lawn and patio areas, should be lined up with the house. Do this by imagining the house sitting in a grid of lines that run through the rest of the garden. Do not make the mistake of aligning features with the garden's boundaries: unless the boundaries are at right angles to the house, it just won't look right (see also pages 46–7).

Use focal points

Focal points are key in garden design, drawing the eye and guiding your journey around the area, encouraging you to explore. Without focal points, the eye will simply move to the end point, which is why they are so effective in small gardens and can help them to appear larger than they are. Placing a simple pot at the end of a view down a pathway is an easy way to create a focal point as it draws the eye towards it. Seats can be used in very much the same way. A comfortable seat at the end of a long pathway not only draws the eye as a focal point but is also an invitation to sit and rest.

In addition to the opportunity to provide a visual pleasure, a focal point can be used to lead you to a different area of the garden. Do this by exploring various lines of sight, or vistas, within the garden and try to plan them so that on walking around the garden they appear in turn. If possible, make the use of the longest possible vista that you can in your garden, and place a focal point at each end. Wherever a path crosses this vista, there will then be a view to something attractive in both directions. These two-way focal points may be seen quite often in public gardens on a grand scale, but the same principal can be applied in your own garden.

You don't need to consider expensive statuary or an architectural structure. A focal point can be created simply by using a container such as a large pot or tub with a mixed planting that can be changed with the seasons (see overleaf).

Plants can make excellent focal points. A choice tree or shrub or perhaps an architectural planting of phormiums or palms, placed at the crossing point of pathways, can lead one to a separate part of the garden or simply provide an uncomplicated distant feature.

If you are fortunate enough to have a space that is large enough for pathways to be incorporated into your overall plan, then you should spend some time carefully planning the layout and direction

Place a focal point at the end of a pathway or steps and your eye will be drawn towards it.

How to create a simple focal point

You can create a simple focal point in your own garden by using a stack of dry bricks, topped by a large terracotta pot. Change the planting in the pot twice a year to keep your view fresh and varied.

1
Make a firm base using a paving slab bedded onto a mortar mix. Check it is level and tamp it down firmly.

2
Lay down the first layer of bricks so that they alternate. There is no need to add mortar to the bricks as this brick pattern is very stable.

3
Build subsequent layers with bricks facing in alternate directions to ensure a firm structure. Continue to add layers to a height of 45cm (18in). Stand your container – or any other focal point (see page 108) – on top.

You will need
- paving slab
- mortar mix
- club hammer
- spirit level
- bricks

The finished focal point, which successfully draws your eye from one garden room into the next.

of the pathways. A single loop around the edge of a piece of land can quickly become boring and feel repetitive. It is a much better idea to ensure that pathways cross each other. One of the main benefits of including this style of walkway in your design is that you will be provided with opportunities for long or short walks through the garden. It will also give an option to see the garden from many angles and prompt you to consider improvements that otherwise may have remained unseen. Paths also split the garden into different sections, which allows you to plan a variety of diverse rooms in the garden.

Create different rooms

Just as you have different rooms in your house, you can use the same principal to create and design different rooms in your garden. A garden divided into several smaller units will be a lot more interesting than one where you can see the whole garden all at once. Divisions using walls, fences or hedges to create these separate rooms will add a sense of mystery to your garden. It's also always a good trick to visually lose sight of any boundaries if possible, especially if your garden is small. The division of the garden space is one way of doing this, but also think about using deep plantings to further disguise the boundaries. By using both of these techniques, the garden will feel much larger than it actually is.

This well-planned garden has been divided to form a garden of rooms – two areas with lawns and a further gravelled area. At eye-level, none of the rooms are seen completely until they are entered, due to the tall plantings used as divisions.

An otherwise direct pathway is interrupted by a container, which also acts as a focal point. Clipped hedges divide this garden into smaller areas, which make it feel larger.

By creating rooms within your garden, you also have an opportunity to give each room a different feel or function. You can walk from an informal area into a strictly formal one. Or contrast a hot sunny area with a partially shaded one with cool-coloured flowers and foliage. Creating different rooms can often solve differences in opinion between yourself and a partner on what you wish from your garden. Perhaps you like soft pastel shades and your partner favours lively vibrant colours – the answer is to have two separate garden rooms reflecting each particular taste. Remember that these rooms in the garden do not need to be square with hedges on all four sides. They are simply distinct garden areas, sitting within the garden as a whole.

Remember pathways

Use pathways to link rooms and to snake and circle around them. When designing your garden, consider using curved paths as well as straight ones. The width of a path can also change its feel completely. Some should be wide enough for a couple to walk along side by side to have a romantic stroll around their garden, while a very narrow path cutting through tall plants can give a sense of adventure and exploration, especially if it curves out of sight. Pathways can be formal or informal, depending on how they are used, their dimensions and the materials employed in their construction. More formal straight paths tend to suggest a feeling of a quick, direct route to wherever they may lead, while a narrow path continually curving out of sight suggests a much slower, more leisurely journey through the garden; these work best through taller plantings so that there is something unknown and unseen about where the path will take you.

Even in your kitchen garden don't feel the need to conform to a straight path dividing your plot. Why not be adventurous and try an S-shaped path through the usually regimental rows of vegetables?

Position a lawn

If you are planning a main lawn area, the shape, size and direction of the lawn can dramatically affect the look of your garden. You can make your garden look bigger or smaller by visually losing or pushing back the boundaries. A long narrow lawn with straight sides will take the eye quickly down to the end of the garden, making it appear longer than it is. A curving lawn that appears to disappear out of sight behind large shrubs has a slower feel to it, and may take the line of sight to a feature tucked away, creating a sense of mystery.

Angled lawns: Rather than the lawn coming off the house at 90 degrees, why not consider turning it to a 45-degree angle? Still use the principal of the house sitting within a grid, but just realign your plans to a 45-degree angle. To decide whether you are going 45 degrees to the left or right, look to see where that would then take your line of sight – ideally to a specimen tree or shrub, or possibly to a feature or focal point such as a favourite piece of sculpture.

Make use of any views out of the garden, too. Look to see whether a neighbour's tree could be used as a focal point in this way. Again, drawing the eye past your boundaries will make your garden seem larger than it actually is. Diagonal lines at 45 degrees to the house

Circular lawns can make an area feel larger than it actually is. Here the borders are thickly planted, which disguises the straight lines of the boundaries, and a carefully sited seat acts as a focal point too.

stretch the garden and make a lawn look less regular, even though it still has straight sides. They also create deep borders in places, giving increased planting possibilities. However, for this to work, remember the whole of the lawn needs to be aligned at this angle.

Circular lawns: A circular lawn has a widening effect, pushing out the feeling of space in all directions. They work well in small spaces as they have a very strong visual impact and they also usually create very deep borders for planting. Deep borders enable taller plants to be used, which, in turn, help to mask boundary fences or walls.

Circular lawns are useful if you create rooms in your garden as they can offer a good contrast to a rectangular lawn and pathways can lead off them at any angle. Seating spaces, too, can more readily be positioned wherever it suits you. A circular lawn is another solution for a small, odd-shaped garden plot – the circle becomes the dominant shape rather than the odd shape of the garden (see page 61).

Plan for storage

There is nothing more annoying than not being able to find a particular garden tool, or, having found it, needing to move garden furniture, hosepipes or bicycles out of the way to get to it. The answer is to first find space for a garden shed, and then organize it!

Siting the garden shed: It is important that you site your shed carefully, both from an aesthetic and a practical point of view. If your shed is far away and difficult to get to, you are not likely to use it as much – but nor do you want it blocking your view. If you have an odd space tucked to one side of the house, this may be the perfect spot. If it is long and thin, two small sheds may be joined together, to fill the space efficiently. Consider, too, having an electricity supply for lighting and charging power tools.

While garden sheds are available in metal or plastic versions, traditional timber sheds are much nicer to look at and are the easiest to disguise or blend into the garden. They can be painted or stained and could have trellis for climbing plants easily attached to them. Rather than trying to hide your shed, it's also possible to build a shed with a façade that looks more like a summerhouse, making it a feature in its own right. Look for a design that complements your house. Apart from the usual selection of garden sheds, it is also possible to build your own from a kit.

Sheds don't need to be brown! This woodstained shed sits comfortably with the restrained colour scheme used in the surrounding plantings.

Other storage necessities: In a larger garden, if space permits, I like to incorporate a utility area, where the washing line, garden shed, oil tank, compost heap and log store can all be out of sight, neatly fenced off from view from the rest of the garden.

It is best to surround a washing line with open-style fencing to ensure the through-flow of air. Logs need to stay dry, so a roof to keep off the rain is essential, as is access for a wheelbarrow for moving them.

Moving on

By working through your plan bearing each of these elements in mind, you will end up with a really useful tool for planning and costing all your proposed work. Keep hold of any different designs and ideas that you may have made during the process, as it can be very helpful to refer back to them. This is especially the case if you find that you need to make some changes while you are putting your ideas into practice.

Garden shapes and solutions

I have found that travelling by train through towns and cities is a great way to get a peek at other people's back gardens! I am always amazed by the vast difference in shapes and sizes of gardens and by how their owners have developed them. The shape of most gardens is dictated by the layout of the houses, with corner plots often having larger gardens, sometimes oddly shaped. Traditionally, terraced or semi-detached houses in a road will have a garden that is long and rectangular, with shared hedges or fences on either side. Houses on curved streets also tend to have irregular shapes to them.

Consider dividing your garden into smaller units, or rooms, for a more interesting result.

Whatever shape your garden is, try to explore all the possibilities. Regard an odd shape of garden as an advantage, it may allow you to create a much more interesting space. It is amazing how changing the proportions of a lawn or patio can alter the feeling of space and harmony within a garden. And for inspiration and ideas, look at as many other gardens as possible. Visit gardens that are open to the public, look at your neighbours' gardens and, of course, do what I do and check out the views from the train!

A long, thin garden

For a long, thin garden running away from the house, the best solution is to divide it into a few smaller, different rooms, but try to create some vistas and focal points too. If dividing into three parts, for instance:

- The space closest to the house may be a dining area with just a glimpse through to the next room.
- This could have a completely different feel to it, being shaded instead of sunny, all one colour of flowers, or all one type of plant.
- The third part to the garden could differ again in feeling, possibly being a more practical area for children to use or for vegetables to be grown in.

This type of layout makes the garden so much more interesting to look at and be in than one long, undivided rectangle. It may be divided using straight lines, rectangles and squares, or use circular areas that are joined together by pathways or made so that they are just overlapping each other.

Using straight lines in a long, thin garden is much more formal and symmetrical; the plantings you make can either strengthen this feel or tone it down. Using circles and curves is much more informal; again the plants that you select and the style in which you plant them can change the feel completely.

A corner plot

A house that sits in a corner plot often has a triangular-shaped garden with a space at the side of the property in addition to one at the rear. This can at first appear difficult to deal with, but by using the principal of a grid coming off the house (see page 53), you can quickly create a more regular-shaped area that relates to the house and sits comfortably in its space.

- Don't worry about creating deep, oddly shaped borders – these are an asset when it comes to planting, as deep borders can be used to create a lush, multi-layered abundance of planting.
- A circular lawn or patio is a good solution for a small, odd-shaped corner plot as the circle becomes the dominant shape rather than the odd shape of the garden. It gives an impression of space and a feeling of unity and calm too. For the best effect, define the shape by edging the lawn with bricks or pavers, and experiment to see how large the circle can be and where to position it within the available space.

A well-designed circular dining area is the perfect solution in this odd-shaped garden plot. The circle draws the eye away from the boundaries and the design is further strengthened by the round table.

An L-shaped garden can be designed to tempt you to walk around the corner to explore what lies beyond.

An L-shaped garden

An L-shaped garden may be given similar treatment to a long, thin garden, dividing it up into smaller compartments or rooms. An 'L' shape lends itself to easily being divided into either two or three parts, the only difference from a long, thin garden being that the last part turns in a different direction. Hidden from view, this might be the natural place to hide away a vegetable garden or a children's play area. Alternatively, if it is something more tranquil that you are after, create your restful haven in this secluded area. Bear in mind, too, that each arm of the 'L' will have a different aspect, which means you can enjoy varied plantings around your garden.

Where your garden changes direction, you can also make play of the new vista by creating focal points running across the end.

- Imagine walking to the apparent end of the garden, to then be pleasantly surprised by an opening into a previously unseen area.
- A focal point, such as a small shrub in a lovely container, will encourage you to walk to the very end of your new discovery.
- Remember to position a second focal point at the other end for when you turn around to walk back.

A small garden

If you only have a small space, don't worry, you can still make some divisions – they just need to be in scale with your space to work well.

- Instead of using walls, fences or hedges, if space permits, use different surfaces to give the illusion of divisions and carefully position a few vertical plants, such as bamboo.

- Trellis planted with suitable climbers also works well in these circumstances, and it can be cut to any size you require.

- If you only have space for a small seating area and a few plants, keep everything simple. Select plants with muted shades, such as pastels or whites, or with a 'quiet' foliage effect rather than bright, jumpy colours that advance (see pages 130–1).

- Think about using perspective to make a small space look larger by, say, dramatically narrowing a path, lawn or patio as it moves into the distance. This will automatically trick the eye into thinking the furthermost end of the garden is further away than it actually is.

In a small space, concentrate more on foliage effect. Here, golden-leaved Indian bean trees (Catalpa bignoniodes 'Aurea'), ferns and clipped box balls create a stunning effect with not a flower in sight.

Typical problems and solutions

Every garden has its difficult areas – steep slopes, wet spots, overhanging trees and eyesores such as dustbins, sheds and washing lines. To any problem there is always a solution, sometimes just needing a little creativity and inventiveness.

Sloping garden

Steep slopes are often the most daunting issue in a garden. Slopes are not easy to walk up or down, and a sloping lawn can be awkward to mow and maintain. Sloping gardens can be landscaped by terracing; retaining walls are necessary, and may be constructed from stone, timber or brick – but this is definitely a job for an expert. This is especially the case where retaining walls are greater than 90cm (36in) high. A large mass of soil behind a retaining wall can exert quite a force, especially when wet. The choice of material should reflect the construction and style of the house and also local materials.

If your garden needs to be terraced, still remember to use the design principles of rooms, focal points and losing your boundaries. For instance, steps will be necessary and these can create a vista and become a feature in their own right. Also use the grid system to align retaining walls to the house, so that the hard landscaping sits comfortably with the building.

Terraced gardens can be stunning and dramatic, with different areas to be discovered tucked away on upper or lower levels. Lawns do not usually work in smaller terraced gardens, but that allows more planting space.

A sloping plot can easily be transformed by creating different levels linked by steps.

Timber decking: If your garden slopes steeply, a deck can be constructed on supports to provide a level area to use. Depending upon the amount of space, steps could then lead up or down onto a second area. In effect, decking can be used to terrace a whole area, with spaces left for planting.

Shady garden

Large trees can provide a sense of maturity and structure in a garden, but usually the area underneath is not very hospitable to growing plants. Depending on the style of your garden there are a few different options, but it is important to view the space as an opportunity for a feature, rather than a problem.

If grass won't grow, the area could have wood chip or gravel as a surface, and a seat may be placed as a welcoming focal point. Some carefully placed large pots will provide planting opportunities for shade-loving plants or you could make a raised bed from sleepers around the tree (see pages 94–7). These are an ideal solution where the quality of the soil is very poor, such as under trees.

If plants are managing to grow in the dry shade under trees, then the answer is to help them as much as possible. Organic mulches are an excellent way to help conserve what little water there may be, and the mulch will gradually be incorporated into the soil and help increase its water-retaining properties.

Astrantia major and many ferns grow happily in partial shade.

Ferns tolerant of dry positions

Asplenium scolopendrium (hart's tongue fern)
Athyrium filix-femina (lady fern)
Dryopteris filix-mas (male fern)

Some plants will manage better than others, and these are usually ones that have originated in woodland habitats. Ferns are a good example. Although many ferns love moist soil, some naturally grow in dry soil under trees so it is important to select the correct variety.

Foxgloves, too, grow naturally in dry soil under trees and, like ferns, give a pleasant woodland feel. Larger, more vigorous hostas, such as *Hosta sieboldiana*, will grow well once established. For new plantings under trees it is important to incorporate plenty of organic matter in the planting holes and also to water new plants well for their first few growing seasons. There are many shrubs, too, that will grow in dry shade, they may never do quite as well as they would in a more open position, but they will still give good results, especially if given a little extra care with watering, feeding and mulching each year.

Trellis is a quick and easy option for a fast cover-up. Plant rapid-growing climbers or scrambling shrubs such as this Solanum crispum *'Glasnevin' for a swift result.*

Unattractive objects

Nobody wants to sit in their garden and look at washing on the line, or a row of dustbins. Firstly, when planning your garden try to site them away from view, but as they need to be somewhere practical and not everyone has space, this is not always possible. Screening of some sort is required, and there are several options.

Planting shrubs: These provide colour and interest and fit into the overall planting scheme. However, they may take several years to grow to the required size.

Trellis: This is easy to put up, but it needs a covering of climbing plants to do its required job. Trellis could be used in addition to a planting of shrubs as a short-term screen while the shrubs are growing.

Brushwood, bamboo or reed screening: These options are useful too. They come on rolls, are quick and easy to put up and are instant, giving much more of a screen than trellis – and plants can still climb over them.

Use timber decking to cover an otherwise difficult area of ground in your garden.

Wire as a plant support: Sheds and garages can have wires or trellises attached to them for climbing plants to be grown up. But some climbers are 'self-clinging', whereby they have little suckers on their stems that stick to timber or masonry (see page 116). Take care if selecting this type of climber as it may eventually grow out of control and invade gutters and the eaves of buildings. I have recently removed all the ivy covering our home as it was doing just this. Contrary to common belief, climbers do not harm masonry walls themselves, but they may damage masonry that is already in a poor state of repair. So try to keep self-clinging climbers for boundary walls only; there are plenty of less invasive climbers and wall shrubs that will do a great job on your home.

Poor or wet soil

Developers of new houses quite often give little thought to the gardens. Many gardens are left with really poor soil, sometimes a mixture of underlying subsoil mixed with a tiny amount of topsoil, and lots of builder's rubble. In these circumstances, it would require the removal of this poor soil and its replacement with a lot of good quality topsoil and organic matter to successfully establish a garden in such poor conditions.

The unique way that timber decking is constructed makes it a real solution to covering poor soil. As it is simply constructed right over the top of a difficult area (even a permanently wet spot can be covered up in this way), erecting decking could save a lot of time and effort. Alternatively, consider incorporating raised beds (see pages 94–7) into your garden design. Once built, they can be filled with topsoil and used for planting anything from large shrubs to low-level groundcover.

If your garden is so damp that it's difficult to control, perhaps the only thing to do is to accept it and start creating a bog garden.

Part 3
GARDEN STRUCTURE

Walls, paths, fences and patios form the backbone of every garden, and it is from this framework that a garden can be developed and planted. Pathways can take you on journeys around the garden so that you can enjoy all of its different aspects. Boundary walls and fences provide privacy and shelter and, together with pergolas and arbours, give height and support for plants, as well as being features in their own right. Living structures made from willow add a softer, more organic feel. Garden structure is a permanent affair, so carefully consider all choices of materials as they need to be practical as well as attractive. After all, you want to show your precious plants off to their best advantage!

Getting started

Whether you are planning a change to all or just to part of your garden, the first practical job is to tackle the hard landscaping. In the garden industry we use the terms 'soft landscaping' and 'hard landscaping'. Soft landscaping refers to the plantings, the use of topsoil and laying turf. Hard landscaping is the construction of walls, patios, fences, pathways and any other building works. It is the hard landscaping that this chapter is concerned with.

As part of considering a new design or layout for your garden, you will have probably decided that you need to create some new hard landscaping features. You could, of course, contract a professional to carry out the work (indeed, sometimes it's essential), but you may wish to tackle the simpler jobs yourself. This will not only save money, but will also give you a greater sense of achievement once you have completed your new garden.

Hard landscaping is not cheap. In fact, the hard landscaping elements in a new garden can easily account for more than half of the total cost, so it's essential that you plan everything properly to avoid any expensive mistakes.

A wheelbarrow is ideal for mixing a small quantity of concrete; but remember to wash it out well afterwards.

Get some help

One of the main reasons to sort out the hard landscaping first is the disruption that may be caused. Depending on how large your project is, you may need to bring in machinery. A mini digger is a fairly straightforward machine to master and can save many hours of hard labour and backache. If you are going to hire any machinery, save yourself money by identifying other jobs in the garden that you can carry out at the same time.

A cement mixer is essential for all but the smallest of hard landscaping work. Mixing mortar by hand is both backbreaking and time consuming. If you have a very large project, it's worth considering buying a cement mixer and selling it when you have finished your project. If, however, you just need one bucketful of concrete for a repair job, then the easiest way to mix it up is in a large wheelbarrow. You can move your wheelbarrow next to your sand and cement, and then simply wheel it to where it's needed!

With machinery or just a fleet of wheelbarrows your garden may temporarily look like a building site, but don't worry, it will soon recover. Do remember to identify any existing plants that may be damaged or in the way and tie back their branches or carefully dig them up. Also move any pots and garden furniture well out of the way to make your workplace as clear as possible, and prevent any possible accidents.

When your supplies arrive, have them delivered as close as possible to where you are going to use them – remember that paving slabs and stones are very heavy. Make sure, too, that as part of your forward planning you have plenty of helpers to hand: hard landscaping tasks are certainly not jobs to be tackled alone.

Well-designed paths can make all the difference to the style and finished look of a garden.

Choosing your materials

The outside of your house will have a particular style and feel to it, and it will impose itself onto your garden. Well-designed gardens take this into account and also take the house's setting into consideration, marrying the two together to create an overall harmonious balance.

Houses were traditionally built only from local materials, and this is what gives older towns and villages their distinctive look. In the English Cotswolds, for instance, the local stone is a warm golden colour, and this is what has been traditionally used for the construction of all the buildings there, giving a particular feel to that whole region. Any new building, whether a garage or house, if built in the same local materials, will instantly blend in with the original architecture. Scandinavian countries, with their extensive timber-producing forests, build mostly timber houses and structures. Timber also works well outdoors, and so for this style of house, timber decking always looks very comfortable as part of the garden landscape. So, by planning to use the same local materials in the construction of the garden, you will help the overall design of the garden to sit naturally alongside the house.

Even if your house is different to its more traditional immediate neighbours (possibly a little more recently built), the material of its surroundings should still be taken into account. For example, if you are in the middle of a 'red brick' area, the red bricks are still part of your local landscape, and if strongly visible from your garden on other surrounding buildings, they will work well as part of your garden style.

Choose wisely: Obviously, the plants that you use in the garden will be a matter of personal taste and suitability for the location. However, the selection of materials you use for any hard landscaping, such as walls, steps, paths and paving, will require planning and thought to ensure they work well with their surroundings rather than stick out like a sore thumb.

Limiting the number of different hard landscaping materials will produce an uncluttered design, especially if they are repeated around the garden; this applies to plants as well, where repetition can bring unity and a sense of order. This is not to say that you should overuse any particular material. In any garden, the plants are the main source of entertainment and visual pleasure.

Good combinations: For a country-style garden, natural materials such as York stone paving, granite sets, gravel and bricks laid in a basketweave pattern would look at home, especially if weathered. A Mediterranean theme could also use gravel together with some larger pebbles, and the use of terracotta or sandy coloured tiles instead of bricks to suggest an authentic, sunny environment. Wood and stone, such as slate, work well together, creating a strong contrast, and look especially good in a contempory urban setting.

The cost

Uppermost in many people's thoughts is how much will it all cost? Typically, installing hard landscaping is the single most expensive part of a new garden design, so think carefully about how large your patio area really needs to be: making it unnecessarily large will just add to the expense. The use of gravel or chippings is much more economical than paving, and much easier to install too.

If you divide your garden plan into individual projects, you can work out the cost of materials for each part. Remember that skilled labour can add quite a lot to your budget, and you can save money by carrying out any simple jobs yourself.

*Regional house building materials (**opposite**) will suggest which hard landscaping materials will look good in your garden. A red brick pathway within the garden of a red brick house, for example (**above**) or local slate (**below**) gives a feeling of continuity.*

Boundaries

As part of the hard landscape in your garden, boundary fences, walls and hedges possibly have the greatest visual impact.

Timber fences range from traditional to contemporary finishes. Choose a style to fit in with your chosen garden design.

If you live in the countryside, your garden boundaries may only really be needed to provide shelter, which gives you the option of leaving some open boundaries to allow unrestricted views out of the garden space. Here woven willow hurdles or woven hazel panels can look charming. However, in an urban setting, it may be more important to deal with the issues of privacy and security. The choice of boundaries is more than just fence panels or a conifer hedge, there are many options to consider, each with its own advantages and disadvantages.

Take for example those conifer hedges that can cause so many problems. The tree in question is the Leyland cypress (x *Cupressocyparis leylandii*) and it is the fastest-growing conifer in the British climate,

managing to grow at the rate of almost 1m (3ft) a year when established. It does seem an attractive proposition when you are in the garden centre – it's cheap, evergreen, very fast growing, and so much easier than erecting a fence. However, its rate of growth and eventual size if not trimmed regularly make it completely unsuitable for any smaller gardens. It is far more suitable for rapid screening of large-scale eyesores such as motorways and factories, in areas where it will have plenty of space to grow. Such is the problem with the Leyland cypress in small gardens that legislation has been introduced defining them as nuisance hedges. Needless to say, it's not a plant I recommend, unless it is trimmed regularly to keep it under control.

These open styles of timber fence have a rustic feel and are also suitable supports for climbing plants. Although the basic design of open timber fencing tends to be the same, the choice of wood and finish can be chosen to fit in with your garden style.

Fencing

A hundred years ago when labour was cheap, most boundary walls were made of local brick or stone. Today this option, while desirable, is far too expensive. The most common boundary material is now timber fencing, with ready-made lightweight fence panels being very popular.

Your choices: Fence panels are most commonly available in two styles: overlap or interwoven. Overlap panels give a little more privacy than interwoven panels and are more pleasant to look at. Alternatively, look to a 'featheredge' or 'closeboard' timber fence, where fence posts are installed as usual and horizontal rails are then fixed to them. The same post and rail structure that is constructed for a featheredge fencing can also be used to create a more informal boundary. If absolute privacy is not an issue, fix vertical timber strips or rustic half round posts to a post and rail structure, creating a rustic-looking fence that can support climbing plants. Trellis can also be a suitable material for a boundary. A custom-made

fence is really useful if you have any awkward turns or bends on your boundaries. You can also make it whatever height you require, just by ordering the appropriate sizes of timber.

Colour: Ready-made fence panels are usually quite a bright colour, and although they are made out of treated timber, the best thing to do with them is to tone them down by painting them with a preservative woodstain. There is only one colour to go for, which is a very dark brown. Don't be tempted by bright blue or the orange tones of red cedar, you will just draw more attention to your boundary fence, when it's the plants we should be looking at.

Trellis is useful as an instant, informal boundary.

Erecting: Unfortunately, ready-made fence panels are fiddly to erect, the posts need to be exacted vertically and the measurements must be perfect. In windy areas they are also prone to damage from strong winds, and are usually not repairable. For something simpler, consider erecting a featheredge timber fence (see pages 78–9).

A more unusual combination of holly (Ilex aquifolium) and purple beech (Fagus sylvatica 'Purpurea') creates a hedge with an interesting tapestry of colour and texture.

Hedging

Hedging is an easy option for a garden boundary, the main drawback being that we are generally impatient and can't wait for it to grow to the desired height. Some specialist suppliers sell extra large plants for instant hedging; they are expensive, but may be worth considering if you only have a small length of hedge to plant.

Your choices: The main choice with selecting plants for your hedge is whether you need it to be evergreen or deciduous, and whether you wish to have a formal clipped hedge or a more informal look. Evergreen hedges such as holly (*Ilex aquifolium*) and yew (*Taxus baccata*) are slow to establish and plants are more expensive, while deciduous

hedges such as beech (*Fagus sylvatica*) and hawthorn (*Crataegus monogyna*) are quicker and cheaper.

For a more informal look, choose shrubs like *Cotoneaster franchettii*, *Rosa rugosa* or barberry (*Berberis thunbergii*), which will provide an informal, lower hedge. Of course, you can plant a hedge out of almost any shrub that you like. Bamboo, for instance, makes an excellent evergreen screen and if your climate is not frost prone, camellias would give you a lovely flowering evergreen hedge. The only difference is the cost, with these types of plants being more expensive, but still worthy of consideration.

Buying: In the autumn, hedging plants are usually available 'bare root', which means they have been grown in rows in a field, and dug up to be sold. As they have not been individually potted up and looked after, they are much more economical to buy.

Before planting: Whatever hedging you choose, make sure you cultivate and prepare your soil well. Dig the soil deeply, and incorporate plenty of well-rotted organic matter. Water the new hedge during dry spells of weather, particularly in its first growing season.

Maintenance: Hedges require regular ongoing maintenance to keep them looking good. Hedges that are faster growing may be quick to reach their desired height but will then need more trimming each year to keep them under control.

*An informal hedge of bamboo in my own garden (**above**) has quite a different feel to a formally clipped yew (Taxus baccata) hedge (**left**).*

How to erect a fence

A featheredge style of fence is much easier to erect than ready-made fence panels, looks good and gives greater privacy too. Although it may initially cost a little more, it is stronger and will outlast traditional fence panels by years. One advantage of this type of fencing is that your posts do not need

You will need

- 1.8m (6ft) high featheredge fencing (ten pieces per metre/yard)
- 40 x 80 x 1800mm (1½ in x 3½ in x 6ft) horizontal rails
- 2.1m (6ft 9in) fence posts (or 2.4m/7ft 9in if you wish to attach a trellis to the top as we did)
- string line
- spirit level
- hardcore, e.g. broken bricks, rubble or pieces of stone
- concrete
- nails
- hammer
- tape measure
- someone to help you!

1
Use a taut string line to mark the line of the fence and then measure and mark the position of the posts, about 1.8m (6ft) apart. Dig holes approximately 40cm (16in) deep.

2
Place a post in position and support it with hardcore. Check that the post is upright, in line and the correct height – there should be 1.8m (6ft) of the post above ground level.

6
To fix the horizontal featheredge boards, start at one end of the fence rails and place the first board in position. Use the spirit level to check it is vertical and nail it in place with a single nail through the thick edge of the board at the top, middle and bottom.

7
Take the next featheredge board and place it so the thick edge overlaps the thin edge of the preceding board by about 12mm (½ in). Check it is vertical and nail through the thick edge of the board as before. Continue along the rest of your fence in this way, checking that your boards are all vertical as you go.

8
If you then want to attach a strip of trellis, rest the bottom of the trellis on the top rail and nail it to what remains of the upright posts.

to be equal distances apart, and while you should try to position your posts as upright as possible, this method is forgiving of any minor mistakes. The main steps with making a featheredge fence are erecting the fence posts, attaching horizontal rails and then nailing on the 'featheredge' vertical boards. Ensure that the wood you buy has been treated for outdoor use.

3
Mix the concrete with an appropriate amount of water (follow the manufacturer's instructions) and shovel it in around each of the posts.

4
Use spare pieces of timber as temporary supports to keep the posts propped up while the concrete sets. Continue with all the posts in the same way, checking that they are upright and in line. Leave for a couple of days for the concrete to fully harden.

5
Fix the top horizontal rail level with the top of the posts (or if adding trellis, leave 30cm (12in) of post at the top). Nail the rail to the posts. The ends of the rails should meet each other in the centre of each post. Repeat with the middle and bottom rails.

The finished featheredge fence. The new timber fence can be darkened in colour, using an appropriate woodstain.

Patios and paths

Installing a paved patio area or a timber deck is a big, but manageable job. Paths, too, can be time-consuming to create. As I have stressed, planning is the key to completing this type of task successfully. On a typical garden design project I find that there are many, many hours of planning and research, often unseen by the garden's owners. But the more planning that is carried out, the smoother the work in progress will be, and the better the end result. The construction of paths is really quite simple. If you are using paving to match your patio area, just lay the path using the same method. See page 84 for constructing a brick path.

*Consider combining paving materials for a touch of variety (**above**); but don't choose too many different finishes. You should also choose your materials to match the house and its location (**below**).*

Paving

Before you go to choose your slabs, mark out the site with wooden pegs and brightly coloured string and measure it out. This will help you to assess how many paving stones you will need. Try to avoid the need for any slabs to be cut as this will save time and avoid you having to hire a stone-cutting machine, which is noisy and unpleasant to use.

Your choices: When we think of paving, we often think of the standard grey concrete slabs, but a trip to a builder's merchant or DIY store will show you a wealth of different designs and materials available. With paving, compromises often have to be made on the use of local materials. In many regions, locally produced stone for paving is just out of reach financially for most people. Remember, though, that you can still take into account what the local stone is, and try to select a modern product that echoes it.

Preparation: Once again, this is the key to success for a new paved area. The base that you lay the slabs on needs to be solid, level and compacted so that it doesn't sink or subside in the future. There should also be a very slight fall across the finished surface of any patio (or decking for that matter) to direct rainwater away from the house or building. Generally, a compacted hardcore base of about 7.5cm (3in) is sufficient, topped with a 5cm (2in) layer of dry sand and cement. The paving slabs are usually laid with a 1–2cm ($^1/_2$–$^3/_4$in) thick blob of mortar under each corner, so if you add the thickness of your paving to these measurements, you can work out how far down you need to excavate to start with. It is worth hiring a vibrating plate to compact the hardcore as this will ensure the base is very solid.

> Look in reclamation yards for second-hand flagstones, which may be within your budget.
> If you are going to have large expanses of paving, consider breaking them up by leaving some gaps for plantings. These could be low-growing carpeting plants. Chamomile (*Chamaemelum nobile* 'Treneague') is a particular favourite of mine, releasing its wonderful pineapple fragrance when stepped on. Creeping thyme (*Thymus serpyllum*) and pennyroyal (*Mentha requienii*) are brilliant too when used in this way. Larger plants can also look good, with evergreen architectural plants being especially effective.

Levels: As you are laying the paving, keep checking the slabs are horizontal with a spirit level (a rubber mallet is useful for tapping the slabs). Lay the slabs like bathroom tiles, leaving a space of 5–10mm (1/4–1/2 in) between each one for pointing with a mortar mix of four parts sand to one part cement. You will also need to consider drainage of rainwater so that it can be directed away from the house. Usually a fall of 1cm (1/2 in) to each metre (yard) is sufficient.

*Changing the direction of the decking timber highlights any change in level (**right**). Recessed lighting (**below right**) can also be used to show where steps and edges are – useful from both a design and safety point of view.*

__Below__: Decking can be inset within another hard landscaping material, creating a rug-like effect beneath a dining table.

Decking

Your choices: Decking is most commonly seen as a grooved softwood, but there are many different widths available and hardwood options, too. Reclaimed timber can give a really individual look, and scaffold planks used as decking can make a really bold, rough-and-ready design statement.

The timber: This can be grooved or smooth but in wet climates, smooth decking needs to be cleaned properly to avoid accidents, as it can become slippery. I usually use a pressure washer a couple of times each year to give ours a really good clean.

Construction: Decking is fairly simple to construct and there are many detailed sources of information on this. However, the most important and time-consuming part of a decking job is the construction of the timber frame that the decking is fixed to. The laying of the decking timbers really does not take very long in comparison to the time spent on building the main structure. Steps and handrails are available, and balustrades are useful too; in conjunction with a gate they can create a safe, enclosed, child-friendly area.

Bricks

Bricks are easy to use for steps, pathways and as edgings. They are an especially attractive option as they can reflect the use of brick on the house, and can be laid in several different patterns. They have a charm of their own and a somewhat romantic feel. A simple brick pathway may link two areas of garden without too much formality, or become a winding path. Bricks also make a good edging for a circular lawn, and repeating them through the garden helps to give a feeling of unity.

Above: Bricks are a versatile material perfect for using on steps, paths and patios. They may be laid straight or curved and also look good combined with other materials. Buy bricks designed specifically for this purpose, or they may shatter in the frost.

Right: I've used traditional granite setts to complement the old farm barn that we live in. The size and circular design of the setts help to create an impression of greater space.

How to make a brick path

You will need
- bricks
- spade
- shovel
- vibrating plate (optional)
- cement
- sharp sand
- piece of flat timber
- rubber mallet
- spirit level
- broom

Bricks have a lovely warm, soft quality about them. Many houses, including ours, have been built using bricks, and repeating them in the construction of the garden gives a sense of harmony between the garden and house. Although it is possible to obtain reclaimed second-hand bricks, it is better to buy new paving bricks that will not shatter or split in the frost. There is a wide range of colours and textures available, some with the appearance of traditional bricks.

Bricks allow for various patterns; laid end to end running down a pathway they will draw the eye quickly along it. Herringbone patterns are more traditional, and if laid within straight brick edges, gaps may be left for planting with low, creeping plants (see below right).

Laying a brick pathway is fairly quick and easy, but before you begin, you must decide on its size so you can estimate how many bricks you will need. As a rule of thumb, you need about 18 bricks per square metre (yard).

1
Mark out the area and, using a spade and shovel, dig out the loose topsoil, working down to a firm base. Use a rake to ensure the surface is level.

2
Spread a level of hardcore onto the base and level. Tamp down the hardcore. If you are making a large pathway, a vibrating plate is worth hiring to do this.

3
Mix mortar to bed the bricks on: use a mix of 1 part cement to 5 parts sharp sand. Spread the bedding mortar to a depth of approximately 3cm (1¹/₄in). Start to bed the bricks onto this, using a piece of flat timber to keep the tops of the bricks level.

4
Check the levels as you go with a long spirit level. After finishing bedding the bricks, make up a dry mortar mix and, using a broom, sweep it into the joints. Sprinkle lightly with water, which will set the dry mix.

KIM'S TIP

> **Don't leave any wet mortar on the top of the bricks as, if it sets, it will be difficult to clean off.**

Gravel and other surfaces

Gravel pathways look pretty and are quick and easy to lay. You will first need to fix in place treated timber edges by nailing them to wooden pegs that have been driven into the ground at intervals. You can buy these pegs from the same place that you obtain your timber edges. If you are making a pathway across soft soil, it is best to excavate and make a solid hardcore base to about a depth of 10cm (4in), before top dressing with the gravel (see opposite).

Use large-grade gravel to discourage cats from using the gravel as a toilet. There are also several different colours of gravel, so try to match it to your existing hard landscaping. For a rough guide on quantity, expect a 40kg (88lb) bag of gravel to cover 1 sq m (10 sq ft).

Locally produced gravel or chippings are usually quite cheap and can be used in combination with paving to keep down costs, and can also provide places for plants to grow. You can easily replace gravelled areas in the future with further paving.

The cheapest pathway is a simple grass one, which can be an extension of a lawned area or just a pathway in its own right. Make them curved or straight to fit in with the style of the garden.

Above: Upright slate stones are used with slate chippings or 'mulch': both materials are likely to come from the same place. Locally produced gravel (below) is less expensive and quick to lay, while grass (right) is the softest underfoot.

Lighting

It is really simple to add greatly to the enjoyment of your garden by fitting some outdoor lighting. For most people it is not an important consideration at the start of the garden design process, but it is worth thinking about as it's much easier to run in some electrical cable before any landscaping has been carried out.

Candles are a simple and inexpensive way of providing light outdoors. Best of all, they add a romantic touch to any garden setting.

Even if you don't think that you will be sitting outdoors late at night, outdoor lighting is still necessary. There needs to be a safe, well-lit route to your front door and also from the house to the garage, shed or log store. Most of us will have some sort of outside light over a door, installed as part of the domestic electrical system, even this can make a difference and help to light the garden a little.

Lighting for safety also doubles up as security lighting, often using infra-red sensors to automatically turn on the lights when people walk into the area. Safety lighting can be quite industrial and far brighter than is comfortable to live with, so it's worth looking at the options for modifying the light fittings – provided that doesn't compromise your security or safety.

Lighting for relaxation

After looking at what lighting is required in your garden for purely practical purposes, the next step is to consider lighting an area where you may sit or relax. There is nothing more pleasant than sitting in the garden on a warm, still summer's night, especially if you have planted some evening-scented flowers. My favourites to plant next to such an area are honeysuckle (*Lonicera periclymenum*), evening primroses (*Oenothera biennis* or *Oenothera odorata*), tobacco plants (*Nicotiana alata*), night-scented stock (*Matthiola bicornis*) or the exceptionally scented *Cestrum parqui*, a semi-evergreen shrub from Chile with yellowish green flowers in midsummer.

Seating areas: There is a wide range of light fittings available from ultra-modern to traditional. If the lighting is switched on and off from inside the house, consider having a dimmer switch fitted, so that the mood and ambience can be changed as required.

Garden features: Some garden features may be worthy of lighting up individually. Focal points such as sculptures, topiary or containers can

*There are endless possibilities for garden lighting. Start by deciding whether your lighting is for purely practical purposes (**below**) or more of a design statement (**right**).*

look really special with a little lighting. Or consider lighting a pathway or large tree to add further interest. I must mention, though, that it's easy to overdo garden lighting, so I would recommend experimenting with it to get the best effect.

Candles: I especially like to use candles outdoors at night: they are cheap, need no wiring and give a surprising amount of light! The ones sold as outdoor candles have a thicker wick to prevent gusts of wind extinguishing them. However, these smoke a little more than standard candles so they should not be used indoors.

Solar lights: These are becoming increasingly popular for use in the garden and with no need for wiring they are installed instantly. However, they are not very bright and are best used just for highlighting the edge of a path or steps.

Installing: This is, of course, a job for a qualified electrician. Some electricians specialize in garden lighting and they are worth consulting for their help and expertise. Outdoor lighting may be either standard mains voltage or low voltage with small transformers. The low-voltage systems are obviously a safer option but with circuit breakers and the use of specially armoured cable, electricity in the garden should realistically present few safety problems.

*There are many different lighting styles available, to suit all tastes and budgets. Some stand alone and are designed to call attention to themselves (**above centre**), while others are more discreet (**left**). In addition, you will need to decide if you want a light that is directional (**left**) or one that emits an all-round, softer light (**above centre**). Take a trip to your local garden centre.*

Water features

I have chatted with many different people about their gardens and one thing that everyone seems to wish for above anything else is a water feature. Water appears to have a particular attraction to many people. We are all constantly drawn to visit the seashore, lakes and rivers. There is just something very peaceful and soothing about the sound of moving water. Just as important to me is the amount of wildlife that water can attract and support in a garden setting. Creating a pool of water in your garden will immediately attract insects, birds and other creatures, even if it is just a humble bird bath. You can also introduce your own fish of course, so if you choose to make a pond, you might want to consider stocking it with some native species of fish as well as enjoying planting its surroundings.

Child-friendly water features can still be interesting. In each of these examples, there is a reservoir that catches the water underneath these features. It is then pumped up to the surface again.

As with other features of your garden, any water feature should be in scale and proportion to the rest of the space, and fit in with the styling too. If you have lots of room, you can make your pond large, but even if you only have a tiny courtyard, it's still possible to incorporate water. A simple water feature or a watertight container with aquatic plants in it, makes a great alternative to a pond. These features take up little space and offer an ideal solution where space is limited.

There are many ways of creating a water feature. Kits are available for many small water features, such as replica millstones and urns, making installation relatively simple. They may be formal or natural, and do not necessarily need to involve a deep pool – an important safety consideration if young children are around. Children can quickly get into real danger if there is water anywhere in the garden, and that includes old buckets or containers. It is an extremely sobering fact that children can drown in as little as 2–3cm (around 1in), so great thought needs to be given when choosing any water feature. Wall fountains and water bubbling over cobbles are probably the safest options, where no still water is accumulating. Grids can be used for

*Floating leaves such as those of these
waterlilies shade the pond and help
prevent the water being turned green
by too much sunlight.*

ponds, which are able to take a child's weight; these are placed just under the water's surface. Any water feature that involves electricity will need installation by an experienced and qualified electrician.

Formal water features introduce an architectural element – many Italianate and traditional Spanish gardens incorporate them. They are ideal for focal points or to help create a vista.

Informal or natural looking water features are more suitable in most gardens. If possible, position a pond in a low-lying area so it looks natural. A sunny spot is essential to keep the pond and its plants growing healthily and for the water to remain clear and sparkling. The only exception is if you have a water feature that only circulates the water to create splashing sounds.

Making a pond

The easiest way to create an informal pond is probably by using a butyl rubber liner. It's then just a matter of digging a hole, removing any stones, lining it with sand, positioning the butyl lining and filling with water. Simple! But make sure you plan your pond properly and allow yourself plenty of time to carry out the project. This will include marking out the shape of the pond (hosepipes are handy for this), creating ledges for marginal plants while digging (approximately 20cm/8in deep), checking the edges are level with a spirit level and removing stones to prevent puncturing the lining before you add the sand and butyl. Only then can you slowly fill your pond with water.

A gently sloping side will allow easy access in and out of the water for frogs, toads and other creatures, and if you want to have fish in the pond, it should be at least 60cm (2ft) deep. And then there are the plants. Oxygenating plants produce oxygen, which stops the water turning green and murky, while plants such as waterlilies that have leaves that float on the surface, shade the water, keep it cool and provide cover for fish.

Floating leaves will also help reduce algae. Aim to have about half of a pond's surface covered with leaves of free-floating plants such as water hyacinths and deep-water plants such as waterlilies. Most ponds will initially be filled with tap water, which is generally alkaline and may contain additives, so it is advisable to let the pond settle for a week or so before adding plants and fish.

Blanketweed (algae) is a common problem in the summer and needs removing regularly. Use a pronged stick and leave the weed next to the pond for a day or two so any aquatic creatures can get back into the water.

Oxygenating plants: Everybody knows about pondweed, sold at every pond plant centre as a bunch of stems. Oxygenating plants release oxygen into the water and in turn help to keep the water healthy and clean. To introduce oxygenating plants, simply drop them into the pond water and they will grow.

Above: *Blanketweed can be a problem in ponds. Remove it with a forked stick, turning it slowly.*
Below: *A simple bird bath made from an old farm trough makes an unusual water feature.*

*Water lilies (Nymphaea) (**above**) are deeper water aquatic plants whereas
candelabra primulas (**below**) are excellent waterside plants, happiest in moist soil,
where they will self-seed freely.*

Floating plants: These also just need to be dropped into the water.
They float and need no soil for the roots to grow in.

Marginal plants: The roots of marginal plants need to be in soil,
either wet and submerged or just moist soil at the edge of the pond.
Marginal plants are those that would usually be seen growing in or
around a natural stream. It is important to have them growing around
a garden pond as they help it to blend into the garden setting by
obscuring some of the pond edges. Although they need their roots to
be in soil, marginal plants live permanently in the water. The depth of
water that they require varies according to the variety.

Recommended aquatic plants

Caltha palustris (marsh marigold)
Eichhornia crassipes (water hyacinth)
Elodea canadensis (Canadian pondweed)
Equisetum var. *japonicum*
Nymphaea (waterlilies)
Pontederia cordata (pickerel weed)
Stratiotes aloides (water soldier)

How to make a water feature

If you would like a water feature, but you don't have much room, or if the thought of digging a hole in the ground and fiddling about with a liner doesn't appeal to you, well why not choose an attractive container and fill it with water instead? This type of water feature is quick and easy to make and poses no danger to children as long as it is kept sufficiently full of plants.

You will need
- any watertight container
- plants of your choice
- bricks and other stones

1
Place your pot into its final position as it will be too heavy to move when it is full of water. Fill your container with water – tap water is fine as you won't be keeping wildlife in it.

2
Position the deep-water aquatic plants first – I used a dwarf water lily. You might need to place a brick or large stone underneath the container so the leaves sit on the surface.

6
For added foliage interest I used a green rush (*Juncus ensifolius*), and then added the four-leaved oxygenating water clover (*Marsilea quadrifolia*). An oxygenating plant is essential for keeping your water feature healthy and the water clear. They rest just beneath the surface of the water.

7
Finally I added a floating aquatic plant, a water hyacinth (*Eichhornia crassipes)*, which although not completely hardy, is worth using as a temporary seasonal plant for the contrasts of colour and form that it creates with the other plants.

We chose an attractive glazed pot to create our water feature, and sealed the drainage holes with a pond repair sealant, available from any aquatic centre. Some containers now come with a plug so you can turn them into a water feature, and some containers, such as half wooden barrels, usually don't have holes when you buy them. The larger the pot you select the better, it will support more plants and be more of a feature.

3
Do not take the plant out of its pot – all the plants that are placed in the water stay in the pots they are supplied in.

4
Position any feature plants – I used *Equisetum* var. *japonicum*, a type of horsetail that has a very strong shape and form. If you find that a plant's container is unstable or floats, weight it down with a stone or two.

5
As a contrast to the *Equisetum* var. *japonicum* I then used a *Lobelia cardinalis* 'Queen Victoria', a marginal plant that has particularly lovely red leaves and scarlet flowers later in the summer.

The finished water feature with Lobelia cardinalis *'Queen Victoria' in full bloom. It is always worth choosing a sheltered position for a water feature to help prevent the water freezing in the winter.*

Raised beds

A raised bed is really a large container sitting on the ground that is used to grow plants in. They are usually made of timber, but they can also be made of bricks, slates, logs, woven willow or hazel and, for all wine enthusiasts, even upended bottles – what a great way to get rid of your empties! Raised beds are often used for growing vegetables in, but can be planted with any type of plant.

A raised bed made from local slate creates a herb garden. Slate was chosen in this instance as it had already been used in the garden for other features.

Organic gardeners will want to avoid timber that has been chemically preserved, but if pressure-treated timber is to be used, then wear gloves and a face mask when sawing. Woods that are naturally resistant to decay include oak (*Quercus*), larch (*Larix decidua*), Western red cedar (*Thuja plicata*) and sweet chestnut (*Castanea sativa*). Eco-friendly wood treatment products based on natural plant oils are available for you to treat wood yourself. Always avoid railway sleepers that have been treated with tar.

There are several good reasons for going to the effort of creating raised beds. If you have very poor soil in the garden, they can be filled with much better soil. The soil in our garden is heavy clay with poor drainage so raised beds were an obvious solution for us throughout the garden. If you wish to grow acid-loving plants, but your garden does not have suitable soil, a raised bed can be filled with lime-free soil, enabling you to grow anything from rhododendrons to blueberries. Apart from anything else, they look good and can greatly expand the planting possibilities in your garden.

One of the principles of raised beds is that as you don't walk on the soil, once you have filled them, you never need to dig them again. This means the soil does not get compacted, drainage is greatly improved and the plants grow much better. Also because there is no need for access to walk between the rows of plants, they can be grown closer together than if they were in a normal vegetable patch. To maintain the beds they just need a light forking over, incorporating more organic matter into them each year. To make it possible not to need to walk on them, the size of the bed is important.

A raised bed made from concrete blocks patterned to look like wood.

This raised bed is made from reclaimed timber. It measures 1.5m square (1½yd square), which makes it easy to reach into the centre.

> If you were making a long raised bed
(see opposite) you would need an extra
stake at about every 1.5m (1¾ yd) on the
long sides for extra stability.

*Good access around raised beds makes gardening
much easier for wheelchair users.*

A good raised bed: They must be small enough for you to be able to easily reach into the middle of the bed from either side, and can be built to any height, ranging from 23cm (9in) to taller beds. These are particularly useful as they save a lot of bending down and a height of 55–75cm (22–30in) is also the perfect height for sitting on the edge when you are tending to the plants. Wind can be just as damaging to plants as extremes of temperature, so if the area where your raised beds are situated, is an exposed one, make plans to plant or erect some kind of shelter. A wide top edge or a seat built onto the top of a taller raised bed (see page 107) will create a practical place to sit while gardening.

Raised beds are particularly good for disabled or elderly gardeners. However, for disabled gardeners, especially, give thought to the width of the pathways between the beds and also the path surfacing.

The shape of the bed: While most people use raised beds to grow their vegetables, the shape and arrangement of your beds can still be a design feature in itself, and make for a more interesting kitchen garden. You can grow almost any vegetables in a raised bed, but if you have the higher raised beds, taller crops like runner beans may be a little difficult to pick!

Positioning: For the best results, raised vegetable beds should be in a sunny spot, and if they are long rather than square, they should run from north to south. Pathways between them should be wide enough for a wheelbarrow to get through easily. Materials to choose for pathways could include bricks (see page 82), slabs, gravel or bark chips. Remember to use a porous membrane under the path to cut down on weeds if using gravel or bark. One thing I like about the raised bed system is that you can tend your vegetables without getting your boots muddy!

How to make a raised bed

Before starting on this project, decide what size you would like your raised bed to be, where it is to go and how it will fit into the style of the surrounding garden. Don't make it more than about 1.5m (2yd) wide, but you can build it to any height. The simplest designs use scaffold planks as sides – as in this project – so are about 23cm (9in) high. To avoid wastage, check which lengths the timber is supplied in, and work out how many pieces you can cut from each one.

1
Remove any turf or weeds from where the raised bed will sit and level the site. Any perennial weeds and their roots should be dug out and removed. Place the timber sides in position.

2
Knock in a stake at each inside corner. We used 50 x 50mm (2 x 2in) stakes and drove them into the ground for at least 20cm (8in).

3
Nail the stakes to the timber frame from the inside out and outside in, supporting the stake as you do this. You could screw them together using brass or galvanized screws.

4
Saw the top off the stake to the height of the timber frame. Repeat this process in the other corners, checking the timber sides with a spirit level as you go.

Fill the raised bed with topsoil and some bulky organic matter, and it's then ready for planting!

Pergolas, arbours and arches

Pergolas are traditionally covered walkways, usually with climbing plants trained over posts or trellis work, while an arbour is normally a sheltered covering for a seat formed by plants that are trained over a framework. However, these two features both vary enormously in size and style and so sometimes there is not much real difference between the two.

A pergola can be a plant-covered walkway leading you to a garden feature such as a seating area.

Pergolas

Pergolas are generally a little more robust and permanent than arbours. Traditionally they would span a pathway, providing a walkway with shade from hot sunshine. They can be used to link together two separate areas, or to create a new feature in its own right.

Pergolas need to be structurally sound as climbing plants can be quite heavy when they reach maturity. The choice of materials should, of course, be sympathetic to the house and any existing garden structures.

Timber is a common choice for a pergola. It fits sympathetically with many styles, it's easy to work with and can be finished in many ways. As with any timber to be used in the garden, it needs to be either hardwood or pressure-treated softwood to make it last.

Brick or stone columns can also be used to support timber top rails, and **metal arches** can work well too.

The pergola itself adds a permanent structure to the garden space but, of course, the plants that are chosen to grow over it can change its feel and style considerably. For a dramatic effect, consider using just one type of plant for the whole pergola. Roses or grape vines would look stunning when in flower or fruit. For a slightly more relaxed and informal look, a mixture of plants can provide a longer season of

Choose a pergola or arbour to reflect the style of your garden. An arbour (**top right**) can be a good use of an otherwise empty corner of your garden. Here, a wisteria-clad arbour provides a shaded spot in which to sit. Wisterias are really good for arbours or pergolas because of the lovely way in which their fragrant flowers hang downward.

An arbour made with Laburnum x watereri *'Vossii'. Like wisteria, it has flowers that hang downwards beautifully, but do be aware of its poisonous seeds, especially if you have children around.*

interest, with different plants flowering throughout the year. The climbing rose 'New Dawn' has lightly scented, blush pink flowers, which are produced continuously all summer. Or for something with evergreen foliage, choose *Trachelospermum asiaticum*. This climber produces an abundance of very sweetly scented, small, creamy-white flowers in the summer and its foliage looks good all year round.

Grape vines (*Vitis vinifera*) give a Mediterranean climate feel to the garden, even when they are just in leaf. The grapes are an attractive bonus and look fantastic hanging down beneath the foliage in late summer. There is an ornamental variety called 'Brant', which has small bunches of black grapes and fantastic autumn colour. You could, of course, select any grape variety, although the black ones are obviously more decorative in fruit. Grapes are hardy plants, they will grow happily even in cooler climates, but sometimes the fruit may be slow to ripen.

And then there is the wisteria, which is one of my favourite plants over our pergola at home. In May and June it is draped with long trails of highly scented lilac-mauve flowers. The foliage is attractive and

*Clematis flowers come in many different colours and sizes. Clematis montana grandiflora (**top left**) and Clematis montana rubens (**top right**) are vigorous growers. Clematis cirrhosa (**bottom left**) and Clematis 'Nelly Moser' (**bottom right**) are smaller varieties that are easier to accommodate.*

fresh-looking all summer, and it often produces a few extra flowers later in the summer too. There are several varieties, usually lilac-mauve in colour, but there are also pink-tinged, pure white and lilac-purple varieties. Always make sure that you buy a named variety of wisteria, which will be a grafted plant. Cheaper wisterias are sometimes seed-raised plants and will probably never flower that well. Japanese wisteria (*Wisteria floribunda*) is less vigorous than the rampant Chinese wisteria (*Wisteria sinensis*), so will need less pruning and support. *Wisteria floribunda* 'Multijuga' has fragrant, violet flowers. I grow *Wisteria floribunda* 'Rosea', which has exceptionally pretty rose-tinted flowers. Lovely.

There are many varieties of clematis, so it is difficult to choose just one! *Clematis viticella* is a species that comes in a few different varieties. They all have very graceful, not too large, delicate-looking flowers. They look good when they creep through neighbouring climbers like roses or wisteria. Most varieties have purple, violet or blue flowers. The variety 'Purpurea Plena Elegans' has long-lasting double purple flowers.

Arbours and arches

If you would like to add a structural feature into your garden, which will also become a focal point, then an arbour or arch is the ideal solution. Most DIY stores and garden centres sell ready-made arbours and arches for you to assemble at home. Willow arbours are also very popular (see opposite). They are easy to make in the winter or early spring from long lengths of freshly cut willow stems. During the summer, the willow stems will root into the soil and sprout leaves. Many of the plants that are suitable for a pergola are perfect for arbours and arches, too – especially roses and clematis.

*Arbours can provide a seating feature in quite a small space (**left**), while simple archways (**below**) give a real sense that you are entering a special area of the garden.*

How to make an arbour

A willow arbour is easy to make and will last for several years. Willow can be bought from specialist suppliers, who are easy to find on the internet. Before using your willow, soak it in water for a few days to make it easier to weave.

1
Make holes 30cm (12in) deep and 20cm (8in) apart around the base of your arbour – these will be for planting the willow stems. Make a second of series of holes outside the first and add extras at the front to give more strength. Fill each hole with compost and water so that it is as saturated as possible.

2
Start planting the willow stems in the first set of holes you made. Cut the base of each stem diagonally and insert into a hole so they are vertical. Fill with more compost to keep the willow securely in place. Repeat with the outer circle, planting the stems diagonally. Water thoroughly.

3
Weave the diagonal stems across the vertical rods, tying together with garden twine where they cross. Loosely plait the front edge canes for strength. Keep your arbour well watered throughout the summer so the willow can become established for you to enjoy your peaceful retreat.

KIM'S TIP

> For added strength, use garden twine where the willow stems cross each other to tie the willow together.

The finished willow arbour, which we made in the winter. By spring, the stems had rooted, giving us a summer canopy of fresh green foliage.

Garden seating

It would be a shame to spend time creating a wonderful garden for yourself, if you then couldn't sit down and relax somewhere in it to enjoy looking at, and being among, your plants. Seating in a garden is largely practical but seats can also be used as focal points. In a tiny courtyard garden, a small bench for two people to sit and enjoy the sun or shade may be all that is necessary, while larger gardens open up more possibilities.

Even the smallest space can offer an opportunity to create a place to sit.

Where to sit?

I like to have a spot close to the kitchen door, to sit and have a cup of tea in the morning, while at other times of the day, different areas can provide seating for lunch, work or entertaining. If you have the room, you should always have a seat positioned to catch the last rays of the evening sunshine.

The most functional use for garden furniture is, of course, a table and chairs to sit and eat meals at, in your outdoor dining area. The size and style should be in keeping with the immediate surroundings, as well as being practical – a large family will require a large table and many seats.

When considering the pathways and journeys around your garden space, as part of developing your design, think about where you may wish to stop and rest, to enjoy a different aspect of the garden, or to sit in the sun or shade. I think it is always nice to have a seating area positioned where the house is out of sight. In this way you can distance yourself, if you wish, from the telephone and other household distractions. For a smaller garden, you might want to consider hiding such an area behind tall plantings or a tree, hedge or some trellis. Try to plan a 'hidden corner' somewhere in your garden for you to retreat to for a time of seclusion.

Your choices: Personal preference and budget will usually dictate what style of garden furniture you choose. Simple timber furniture usually fits into most styles of gardens, although a contemporary style garden calls for something a little more modern. Here, metal or wood-and-metal furniture would work well.

Garden seating varies a lot in style and can be chosen to match your own preferences. Many traditional seats are constructed from metal or timber (**above** and **right**). However, these materials can also be used to make contemporary styles (**above right**), as with this wonderfully crafted driftwood and steel seat.

Don't underestimate the importance of several seating areas in your garden – you can then really enjoy each different view.

A traditional hammock strung between two sturdy trees is a lovely inviting sight in the summer. Just as your indoor living space needs various pieces of furniture in several places and for different functions, so does your outdoor living space. So try to give a little thought to where you can place some seating for best effect.

If your budget is tight, try looking in second-hand shops and reclamation yards for unusual garden seating. I have seen old railway platform seats and seating from boats put to use in the garden. Or have a go at constructing something yourself – a short piece of scaffold plank on two neat piles of bricks is better than nothing at all. A garden I was recently involved in designing had a recycling theme and old tyres and scaffolding plants made some truly funky benches (see the photograph above).

You will need
- a scaffold plank
- 2 short pieces of treated 150 x 25mm (6 x 1in) timber
- screws and a screwdriver
- compass and pencil
- jigsaw
- sandpaper

How to make a seat on a raised bed

A raised bed is an ideal place for a seat in the kitchen garden, especially next to some aromatic herbs. It provides a welcome place to rest from the weeding or just to sit and enjoy a cup of tea. We decided to make a simple seat and fixed it to the top edge of a raised bed – it's amazing what you can make with an old scaffold plank rescued from a rubbish skip!

1
Decide how long you wish your seat to be and cut your scaffold plank to make two pieces of this length. We made ours 1m (1yd) long and two people can comfortably use it. Check to see which side of each plank is the best, and make these the top of your seat.

2
To make rounded back corners, use the compass and pencil to draw a curve. Then use the jigsaw to carefully cut around each line. We also used the jigsaw to take off the sharp corners on what will be the front of the seat.

3
Place the two pieces together on a flat surface, with the top sides down. Place the treated timber pieces on top. They need to be set back from the front edge of the seat by the width of the raised bed timber. Screw down onto the seat timbers so they securely join together the two halves.

4
Turn the seat over and use the sandpaper to round off all the edges smoothly, and sand the surface of the seat to remove any splinters.

5
Finally, place the seat in position on the soil and screw the front of it onto the raised bed timbers, to keep it firmly in place. Put the kettle on and enjoy your new seat!

Hardscape decoration

After spending time on the pathways, patios and focal points of your garden, it's lovely to be able to think about the more decorative aspects. Historically, sculpture has always been present in gardens, often used rather formally and on a grand scale to mirror the architecture and scale of the property. Today, there is a renewed interest in sculpture, and sculpture gardens and parks are increasingly popular.

Architectural plants such as this Cordyline australis *'Purpurea' have such a strong form to them that they are almost sculptures themselves.*

A garden cannot just be filled with any sculpture though, there needs to be a site in the garden that calls for it, as correctly placed sculpture has far more impact and effect. Sculpture does not need to be the archetypal classical or modern piece either; it may be a large container, empty or planted, or even a striking piece of driftwood.

What is important is that it is:

- Correctly sited
- To scale and in keeping with the style of your garden
- A piece that you like!

Sculptural objects may be statues, sundials, large pots or more contemporary works of metal, stone, plastic or fibreglass. But while many of us may long for a piece of sculpture for our garden, not everyone can afford to buy such items. With a little imagination it is possible to create something yourself. The first thing you need is some inspiration and ideas, and visiting a sculpture park is an excellent start. Andy Goldsworthy, for instance, has created some very simple but stunning sculpture out of stones, and although you may not share his talent, why not be inspired and try something yourself? Large pieces of driftwood are also becoming more popular as garden sculpture. Some are imported and quite expensive, but if you live near a beach, you could go out and look for a piece yourself.

Pots themselves can be sculptural, even new ones. A row of identically planted pots placed in the right position can look great. Also consider filling empty pots with something more unusual. Pine cones, bunches of willow stems, pumpkins or ornamental gourds would all look fantastic.

Whether you buy a sculpture or make something yourself, try putting it in several different places in the garden to see where it works best. Wherever you position it, it's likely to be a very strong focal point. And remember – just like the ornaments in your home, sculptures can be moved around, dressed up with seasonal decorations and changed occasionally too.

Timber, slate and even terracotta forcing pots each have their own sculptural feel. Wherever you position them, think about the surrounding plants – textural contrasts are important.

Part 4
GARDEN PLANTS

The stars of a great garden are undoubtedly the plants and it is from your plantings that you will draw the most enjoyment. The choice of different kinds of plants is immense so I have set out to simplify as best I can the principles of good planting to help you in your plant choices. It is here that you will embark on a life-long learning course, building your knowledge and gaining personal confidence in your gardening ability along the way. Before you know it, you'll have a garden filled with your favourite plants, and I always think that this is like having a garden full of friends.

Let the plants do the talking

How you use plants in your garden has a dramatic effect on the overall look and feel of your garden space. Whether you are replanting your garden from scratch or selecting a few new plants to add in to an existing planting scheme, it is important to understand that different types of plants will have very different and varied influences. Remember that plants are not only chosen for colour and flower. Their size, shape and texture must also be taken into account. These are all differences that you can – indeed, should – use to excellent effect when planning the planting schemes in your garden.

When I started gardening, how to create an effective planting by deciding which plants to group together completely mystified me. I just couldn't get my head around it at all. My initial attempts at creating a cohesive planting scheme that looked as though it had appeared naturally, resulted in a whole avenue of artemisia! Although this did have its charms, it was far from what I was really trying to achieve.

I also didn't want to see any of the soil as I wanted the earth to be covered (I later discovered that this was called groundcover), to stop the weeds taking over. I wanted a scene that would change throughout the year, providing continual interest, while at the same time using plants that wouldn't need too much labour and attention (i.e. it needed to be low maintenance). Ironically, after a good deal of labour and attention, I now have the border I originally wanted, with a backbone of evergreen clipped box balls, some groundcover geraniums, romantic pink *Rugosa* roses and blue nepeta that spills onto the path softening the edges. This has been achieved through a willingness to try things out and learn from the experience. You can do this too. Once you have gone through the early years of the learning curve, your confidence will swell and your experience will provide you with a fountain of retainable knowledge that will mould you into a seasoned gardener.

Other areas of my garden are far more high maintenance, but that is my choice. It's no good having a garden that you can't keep up with as it will only become a chore. The whole world of gardening is one to be enjoyed, so think carefully and plan something that suits your lifestyle and the time you have available to attend to things. Above all, take pleasure in your plants!

This is a view from inside my house of my low-maintenance border, which was my design learning curve (see main text, right). In the distance is a focal point sculpture we call Gandalf, who appears to be walking up the field to greet us.

Planning your planting

It helps enormously if you plan some structure and order into your planting design. Otherwise, matters can easily descend into disorder and confusion. You wouldn't buy a sofa unless you knew you had the right place for it; the same should apply to plants.

A simple but effective way to think about things is to consider your garden as you would consider your house. Follow the steps below and they will help simplify how you plan your planting. Moving in the big furniture and painting and decorating are essentially ways of defining or obscuring your garden's boundaries, and should be considered before anything else. Once that basic framework is in place, then all other planting can be considered. Just one thing though: you will notice in the list that the order in which you would approach decorating a house is slightly altered once outside... but that's exterior planting design for you!

Most plants for garden use may be broken down into a number of different categories: trees, shrubs, climbers, perennials, annuals, biennials and bulbs. When selecting plants it helps to understand the different types and their best uses.

1 Move in the big furniture

These will be mostly trees, evergreen shrubs and hedges. They will ultimately become solid features of the garden and be the 'anchor' for the rest of the planting scheme. They can also be used to provide privacy from neighbouring properties or shelter. Use them as part of your design concept to create separate 'rooms' within the garden.

It is very important to get the overall structure, or backbone, of your garden just right. Everything else will follow from this basic skeleton. Structure will be formed and created by making use of trees, evergreen shrubs and hedges.

Trees: Consider carefully the positioning of any trees. While some of them can be controlled by trimming and pruning, it is much better to select the right variety in the first place. Some trees will grow very large eventually and may cause problems. If space is an issue, choose smaller growing varieties. Make sure that you know the eventual size of your tree, and its rate of growth. While a tree is an attractive background to any planting scheme, you don't want it to dominate too

Large evergreen shrubs provide the backbone to your garden. Here, a Viburnum tinus *gives a structure and maturity to this border that last all year round.*

much. You should also bear in mind the shade that it will create. This might have a bearing on whether you choose an evergreen or deciduous tree.

Do not plant trees too close to your, or your neighbours', house; even a small tree could eventually cause subsidence or even drainage problems. If a tree is allowed to outgrow its available space or grow to an extent that it is causing problems to your property or adjoining property, then it is likely that professional help will have to be hired to solve the problem. This will be costly and probably inconvenient.

Evergreen shrubs: These are often slow growing, and are therefore generally easier to manage than trees. Every garden should have its share of evergreen shrubs. When most other plants have died down and disappeared for the winter, the evergreens give a pleasing sign of continual life in the garden.

Position them in borders as punctuation points. A mature shrub will be noticeable indeed, so ensure they are not positioned too closely together (it is especially important that you remember this when planting them from new – they won't always be that small). You should also plant them with the overall balance and shape of the border in mind, with the taller ones to the back.

Hedges: The choice of shrubs that are suitable for hedging is substantial, so again careful thought is required when choosing. Clipped hedges are useful for the division of gardens into smaller sections or rooms. Hedges, of course, require regular clipping, particularly faster growing ones. However they are perfect for creating the structure that every garden needs (see pages 15–16).

2 Paint and decorate

Look at your garden's vertical surfaces – boundaries, free-standing frames, hedges, trees. Do you have an unsightly fence? Is there a view that you want to obscure? If so, this is the time to consider using climbers, which can be so useful in providing a 'green' screen. When crawling up a surface, climbers help to soften hard edges and provide cover, colour and flower and, most importantly, they add a vertical dimension to your garden. In this respect, climbers are your wallpaper or emulsion! Of course, there is the colour to consider too – more of this on pages 130–7.

Different climbing methods: Climbers attach themselves to walls, fences or sometimes other shrubs and trees, and they do this in surprisingly differing ways.

Self-clinging climbers: Some climbers such as the climbing hydrangea (*Hydrangea petiolaris*) are 'self-clinging'; they have small aerial roots or sucker-like pads that stick them to a support, enabling them to climb without any extra help.

*Climbers such as this Boston ivy (*Parthenocissus tricuspidata*) are called 'self-clinging'; they naturally cling to walls using tiny pads or aerial roots.*

Climbers for a quick cover-up

Actinidia kolomikta
Akebia quinata (chocolate vine)
Clematis
Eccremocarpus scaber (Chilean glory vine)
Lonicera periclymenum (honeysuckle)
Parthenocissus tricuspidata (Boston ivy)
Passiflora caerulea (passion flower)
Solanum jasminoides 'Album' (potato vine)
Vitis coignetiae (ornamental grape vine)
Vitis 'Brant' (grape vine)

Vitis coignetiae is a dramatic climber originally from Japan. It climbs using tendrils so it needs the support of trellis or wires.

Groundcover plants for dry shade

Ajuga reptans 'Jungle Beauty' (bugle)
Euphorbia amygdaloides var. *robbiae* (Mrs Robb's bonnet)
Galium odoratum (sweet woodruff)
Geranium macrorrhizum
Lamium galeobdolon 'Florentinum' (yellow archangel)
Lamium maculatum 'Roseum'
Persicaria bistorta 'Superba' (bistort)
Symphytum ibericum
Vinca major (greater periwinkle)
Vinca minor (lesser periwinkle)

Twining stems: Other climbers, such as honeysuckle *(Lonicera periclymenum)*, have twining stems that wind around any support they come into contact with.

Tendrils: Passionflowers, grape vines and sweet peas are slightly different again, they have tendrils that grab and wind around anything that they touch.

The reason that climbing plants exist is that in their natural habitat they may have been in a shady environment, such as woodland, and they have evolved so they could climb into the tree canopy to reach the sunshine, and then be able to attract pollinating insects, and reproduce.

Giving support: Climbers are capable of putting on a lot of growth very quickly, and while we can make use of this for screening, they may need some extra help to attach themselves to a support (see page 67).

Planting: When planting climbers against buildings, walls (or, indeed, trees), position the rootball away from the wall and then lean the plant in towards the wall. The reason for doing this is that the immediate area next to a building or wall is often permanently dry, some people refer to this as a 'rain shadow'. Give your climbers a really good start by improving the soil with plenty of organic matter when planting (see page 30).

3 Put down the carpet

Quite apart from providing an area of plant interest in its own right, groundcover planting suppresses weeds. This reduces the maintenance required in the garden and will help to show off the furniture (sorry, shrubs!). Groundcover plants are typically ones that spread quickly to form a thick mat of growth; they usually spread by new stems growing outwards from the original plant and rooting where they touch the soil. Depending on the variety, they may eventually colonize a sizeable area. Apart from being useful for weed control they may also be used to stabilize sloping areas of soil.

Many groundcover plants will manage in shade as in their natural habitat they are woodland floor plants. Apart from these natural colonizing plants, many perennials (see page 121) that are clump forming may also be used as groundcover. They should be planted together in a large group, and divided and replanted if necessary so that they quickly grow together into one large mass.

A carpet of groundcover perennials will suppress weeds and look good too. When established, this is a labour-saving style of planting (***above***). Herbaceous perennials such as lady's mantle (Alchemilla mollis) (***above right***) and geraniums (***right***) can be planted in large groups to create dramatic blankets of vibrant colour.

4 Install the fireplace

Focal point plants are the 'specimens' in the garden and should provide some visual splendour in the overall layout. They usually have a well-defined shape and look good all year round. They don't necessarily have to be evergreen, but they do require a strong shape. They undoubtedly should make their presence felt.

Focal point plants are important in a garden of any size, and using a shrub with a distinct shape can be as effective as the use of a sculpture

Shrubs, such as these Cupressus sempervirens, *clipped into bold shapes make ideal focal points. This method of training is called topiary and has been practised for hundreds of years.*

or container. It is often a much cheaper option too. Bold foliage shrubs such as Japanese aralia (*Fatsia japonica*) or bold shapes such as clipped box balls would work well as they have an architectural quality to them. They help to anchor informal areas of the garden and can provide a visual full stop to a view. Most architectural plants happen to be shrubs, often evergreen so that they perform their function all year round. My favourite ornamental grass, giant feather grass (*Stipa gigantea*), which I've used as a focal point plant around my garden, has tall stems and seed heads, which extend interest well into winter.

5 Add a vase of flowers

Ornamental or decorative planting is mostly found in perennials, annuals and biennials and bulbs. They form the decorative details in the garden, being very showy (albeit sometimes only for a brief period), and very colourful. In fact, they are the icing on the cake. As these plants tend to lose their leaves (i.e. they are deciduous) and die back in the winter, they can only ever be additions to the overall structure of your planting plan, but a garden without these colourful delights would be a bare place indeed. Some trees and shrubs also provide splashes of interest, in the form of autumn colour, berries, flowers, coloured foliage or stems.

Crocosmia 'Lucifer' (**right**) *gives an intense explosion of colour in midsummer, other herbaceous perennials, such as day lilies* (Hemerocallis) (**below**) *offer a different range of colour, but all give a wonderful floral display.*

Perennials: Perennials are worth every penny that they cost as they live from year to year and, if happy, will increase in size annually too. While they may take a little more effort to look after than shrubs, their floral display is often spectacular. Try to select perennials that are self-supporting as staking is a time-consuming and fiddly job. Perennials work well at the front of a shrub border, with the shrubs providing the year-round structure and the perennials providing extra seasonal colour. Take time to consider which shrubs will be in flower at the same time, and how the different colours can complement or contrast with each other.

Annuals: Annuals are great for filling in gaps while you are waiting for shrubs to grow, and can temporarily give quite a different feel to the garden. Some annuals fit in well to herbaceous borders, looking more like herbaceous perennials than bedding plants. You might also consider leaving a permanent space in your bed for annuals, so that you can change your plantings with the seasons. I particularly like to use opium poppies (*Papaver somniferum*), spider flowers (*Cleome spinosa*) and tobacco plants (*Nicotiana*). Poppies are easy to grow simply by scattering a packet of seed on the ground where you wish them to flower, and I buy cleome and nicotiana as plants from the garden centre. They quickly grow into fairly tall plants, flowering until the first frosts. For a list of easy-to-grow annuals, see page 166.

*Annuals such as opium poppies (*Papaver somniferum*) (**below**) and sweet peas (*Lathyrus odoratus*) (**right**), grow from seed, flower and then die all in one season. They typically produce masses of flowers as they are trying to produce as much seed as possible.*

Biennials: Wallflowers (*Cheiranthus cheiri*), honesty (*Lunaria annua*) and foxgloves (*Digitalis purpurea*) are all biennials, which means they normally only produce foliage in their first year and then flower in their second. Biennials can be used in the same way as annuals, but the main difference is that they are frost hardy so they stay in the ground during their first winter, then flower in late spring the following year. Honesty and foxgloves are both great 'self seeders', providing new plants that you can allow to grow on and give you even more flowers the following year.

Bulbs: I am sure that we all know what a welcome sight daffodils and crocuses are at the end of a long winter – a lovely splash of colour telling us that spring is in the air. Plant early flowering bulbs among herbaceous perennials. They will flower before the perennials and the bulbs' yellowing leaves will be hidden as the perennials grow. Choose taller flowering bulbs such as alliums, camassia or tulips and mark where they are with canes so as not to inadvertently damage them with a hoe or spade. Smaller bulbs, such as crocus, snowdrops and cyclamens, can be left to increase (naturalize) under deciduous shrubs or in grass, where they are less likely to be disturbed. When planted in a suitable place, your bulbs should multiply and spread year after year.

KIM'S TIP

> When choosing bulbs select the largest ones, and plant them as soon as possible after buying them.

*Hollyhocks (*Alcea rosea*) (**below**) and wallflowers (*Cheiranthus cheiri*) (**right**) are biennials that may sometimes surprise you by lasting for more than two years.*

Bulbs can extend the season of interest in many parts of the garden. Some, such as lilies, do well in pots and can be moved onto patio areas or closer to the house when they are in flower and removed again as they fade. Likewise, spring-flowering bulbs can be used in bedding displays, and carefully transplanted to a permanent position after flowering.

It is very tempting to buy bulbs when you see them filling the shelves at your local garden centre, but, as with any plants, try to plan your purchasing rather than making impulse buys. Think carefully about the flower colours and bear in mind which neighbouring plants may be in flower at the same time.

However you are using your bulbs, it's important to allow the leaves to remain and keep growing for at least six weeks after the flowers have faded. At this point the bulb is building up its energy for flowering the following season. If the bulb's leaves are cut off, it will not flower, or flower very poorly, the next year.

I particularly like to plant bulbs in long grass, where they can remain undisturbed and provide a wonderful show every season. When planting in this naturalistic style, scatter your bulbs across the ground and plant them where they land. This will avoid any regimental look.

*Tulips (**below**) and narcissus (**right**) are two of my favourite spring-flowering bulbs. Tulips come in such a wide range of colours it is possible to fit them into almost any colour scheme.*

Form and texture

When starting the process of selecting new plants for your planting scheme, try not to worry about flowers and colour in too much detail at the start.

Form

First consider the overall shape of a plant (form) as this is the most immediate visual attribute of any plant. Among other shapes it could be:

- Bell-shaped, e.g. rhododendron (left)
- Columnar, e.g. *Juniperus scopulorum* 'Skyrocket' (Rocky Mountain juniper) (below left)
- Spiky, e.g. *Rheum palmatum* (Chinese rhubarb) (below centre)
- Fan-shaped, e.g. miscanthus (below right).

Plant form has great visual impact. In a garden designed for quiet contemplation, choose the miscanthus; the rheum would add drama.

Municipal planting in shopping areas are good places to see how plants with differing forms work together. Often you will find the fan-shaped New Zealand flax (*Phormium tenax*) contrasting with rounded hebes and horizontal cotoneasters.Planting in groups where the shapes are the same can be very effective too .

The difference in foliage texture is incredible. Leaves can be smooth, glossy, dull, matt, jagged or hairy. Planting varieties together whose texture and form are different will create stronger contrasts in your plantings, and even without using any flowers.

Texture

This refers to the size (small, medium and large), shape and surface of a leaf. For example, *Cotoneaster horizontalis* (top left) has tiny, shiny green leaves while *Cotinus* 'Grace' (bottom centre) has larger rounded leaves that are matt purple. Have a look around your garden at the different textures of your plants and you will be amazed at the variety. Now consider how they complement or contrast with each other.

*Plants that have a very strong jagged growth habit, such as these cardoons (Cynara cardunculus) (**above**), are referred to as being 'architectural'. Ferns (**right**) are a good contrast to many other plants, such as these hostas.*

Habit

When considering form and texture, you also need to take into account the habit of a plant. This refers to its characteristic growth pattern. For example, irises have an upright growth habit, while the groundcover plant lady's mantle (*Alchemilla mollis*) has a spreading habit. Many plants have strong habits, such as the upright ornamental grass *Stipa gigantea* or the contorted willow (*Corylus avellana* 'Contorta'), whose twisted stems look especially beautiful in the winter.

Many plants with strong habits are suitable for focal point planting, include the graceful *Cornus controversa* 'Variegata', whose tiered horizontal branches look equally beautiful without foliage, and weeping trees and shrubs such as *Betula pendula* 'Youngii' and *Buddleia alternifolia*. These plants help to punctuate the planting scheme, helping to guide the eye and forming the lynch pin of any design. A garden could have one main focal point, or several spaced around the garden, but be careful not to have too many clamouring for attention in one place.

Plants such as New Zealand flax (*Phormium tenax*), cardoons (*Cynara cardunculus*) and palms have such a strong visual shape that they contrast very successfully with most other plants. But use them carefully in a planting scheme as they tend to dominate. It is this architectural quality that also means they are suitable as focal point plants in their own right. For other plants that have a strong habit, see the list on page 120

Weeping trees and shrubs have a graceful, flowing feel. This weeping pear, Pyrus salcifolia 'Pendula', is a good choice for small gardens.

Some strong combinations ...

Choosing plants for their form, texture and habit before any colour considerations may seem a little clinical, but the end result will speak for itself. Practise looking at plants and noticing these qualities, making a mental note of ones that contrast in a pleasing way.

Imagine your plantings: Think of them as if they were photographed in black and white. This is an easy way to understand how many different foliage types there are, and how to arrange them for the maximum contrast. So take black-and-white photographs of your garden or change them to black and white on a computer. Look at the many different shapes and also the contrast between them. By re-arranging what is already there and adding new varieties, you can create groups of plants with more distinctive differences between neighbouring trees, shrubs and perennials.

Do this, and individual colours become less important. The planting scheme shown on these pages is one I have designed in my own garden, where the strong, rounded form of a clipped box plant (*Buxus sempervirens*, top left) contrasts with the fan-shaped form and graceful, matt green foliage of the shield fern (*Polystichum setiferum*, left). An oak-leaved hydrangea (*Hydrangea quercifolia*, below left) provides a further contrast with its large, bold foliage. These three plants each look good on their own, but placed together they contrast strongly with each other (right). The large, bold, somewhat spreading leaves of the hydrangea are quite different in form to the ferns and also to the clipped box. The result is a successful planting combination, even though the only colour is green, because the beauty lies in the play of contrasting form and texture from each individual element.

Colour, colour, colour!

Following my design principle of decorating a room, here we have at last reached the final part – choosing the colour of your furnishings, carpets and walls. After carefully working your way through the design and layout of your garden, its structure and balance, and the form and texture of different planting elements, this part is like getting out a box of brightly coloured paints and happily splashing them everywhere.

But before you start, there is, of course, some planning to do. I don't want to dampen your enthusiasm, but that lovely splash of bright red may only last a few weeks, so it is important to employ a few tricks to make the most of any colour that there is, and also use it as part of the overall design of the garden.

Colour creates different moods. In the same way that we get feelings from interior design colours and even the clothes that we choose to wear, the colours that we use in our garden will create various emotions. Think about each area within your garden and how you will use it. Bright and hot colours could be used for where the kids play, while cooler coloured plantings could be in an evening area.

Hot colours shout 'Look at me!' and are jumpy and active.

Cooler colours are more neutral, calming and soothing.

When we think of colour in the garden we are usually drawn to thinking of the brightest primary colours: red, blue and yellow. These are the strongest colours and carry the most impact. The secondary colours, purple, orange and green, are equally stunning and have

some shades that are more pleasing and easier to use in planting schemes. Of course, flowers themselves come in many more colour combinations than these main colour groups. There are innumerable shades and tints of the main colours, and sometimes the slightest hint of pink on a white flower can change its feeling completely.

Strong, vibrant colours tend to 'advance' in our field of vision and should be carefully placed, while paler shades will appear to recede. For this reason, a haze of blue flowers placed at the back of a garden can make the depth of the plot seem much longer, while placing bright orange flowers there would make it seem shorter.

Nature paints its own pictures with certain colours. Autumnal landscapes can be fantastic with leaves dramatically turning to bright shades of red, orange and yellow. Wild flowers create swathes of colour in meadows and grasslands, and bluebells can carpet a woodland floor with a sea of blue flowers. Do not forget the colour green either, for it is the green foliage of most plants that sets off the colourful flowers perfectly.

The time of day and the quality of light also affect the way we perceive colour. As the sun's rays redden in the evening, the stronger red colours glow in the dusky light and purples, too, look completely different. White flowers look amazing, they almost seem to glow.

So, when selecting new varieties of plants and planning your colour scheme, do try to explore all the colours that are available. Plants such as roses, for example, have hundreds of different colours from which to choose. Many perennial varieties come in several colour options too, and some shrubs have varieties with different coloured leaves.

Hot colours range from the bright red of field poppies to the strong orange of these lilies and the bright yellow Calceolaria. *Cooler colours include greens and the soft blue of lavender and campanula. Colour is a matter of personal choice but understanding how colours work together will help you to arrange your plants to their best effect.*

The colour wheel

The primary colours are red, yellow and blue and they can't be created from any other colours.

The secondary colours are orange, green and purple and are formed by mixing together two primary colours. The colour wheel illustrates these colours, and how they are related.

Complementary colours appear opposite each other on the colour wheel - red and green, for example.

Harmonizing colours appear next to each other on the colour wheel - orange and yellow, for example.

If you already have an assortment of shrubs and perennials in varying colours, look at how they work together. Introducing another colour next to an existing shrub can dramatically alter the colour effect. Experiment by cutting some flowers or foliage from another shrub, or from perennials, and place them next to it to see how the colours alter. Coloured foliage too is a great tool for extending the season of colour in the garden. Many shrubs have golden, white variegated or purple-leaved varieties and silvery grey leaves occur on many plants too.

I like to plant with groups of colours that are next to each other on the colour wheel. For example, purple echinacea with blue echinops and reddish pink *Sedum spectabile* work well together. The colours blend together perfectly and are gentle and pleasing to the eye. Purple *Verbena bonariensis* self-seeds all around my garden, and looks great among this particular combination of colours. By contrast, planting in groups of complementary colours from opposite sides of the colour wheel, results in colours that set each other off to the maximum effect. They make each other seem brighter.

In my tropical garden area I have used a lot of hot colours - *Crocosmia* 'Lucifer', hemerocallis and cannas all provide wonderful reds and oranges and they are offset perfectly by the lush foliage of bananas, palms and bamboo. Colour comes too from the reddish purple foliage of the smoke bush (*Cotinus* 'Grace'). The hot colours are lively and even jumpy, and they crave visual attention. They are stimulating rather than relaxing, but they work together very effectively.

As a complete contrast to this, in a nearby shaded courtyard area I have concentrated on cool whites and green foliage. This has a much more calming effect, and makes it the perfect place in which to sit and relax on a hot day.

The colour wheel comprises three primary colours – red, yellow and blue – and three secondary colours – orange, green and purple. The secondary colours lie between the primary ones as each is created by mixing together its adjacent primaries. Opposite each colour is its complementary colour and harmonizing colours are next to each other. Understand the colour wheel and you can use it to great advantage when planning your planting.

Top ten colourful plants

Top ten red plants

Fuchsia 'Riccartonii'
Dahlia 'Bishop of Llandaff'
Geum 'Mrs J. Bradshaw'
Hemerocallis 'James Marsh' (day lily)
Lobelia cardinalis 'Queen Victoria' (cardinal flower)
Malus x *robusta* 'Red Sentinel' (apple) (fruit)
Photinia x *fraseri* 'Red Robin' (foliage)
Potentilla fruticosa 'Red Ace'
Rosa 'Geranium' (rose) (fruit)
Rosa 'Falstaff' (rose)

Dahlia *'Bishop of Llandaff' has vibrant red flowers.*

Top ten orange plants

Azalea 'Spek's Orange'
Berberis thunbergii (barberry) (foliage and berries)
Buddleja globosa (butterfly bush)
Crocosmia x *crocosmiiflora* 'Emily McKenzie' (montbretia)
Eccremocarpus scaber (Chilean glory flower)
Hemerocallis 'Mauna Loa' (day lily)
Kniphofia 'Tawny King' (red hot poker)
Potentilla fruticosa 'Sunset'
Pyracantha 'Orange Glow' (firethorn) (fruit)
Rosa 'Crown Princess Margareta' (rose)

Calendula *'Orange King' adds a bright orange glow.*

Top ten yellow plants

Hemerocallis flava (day lily)
Hosta 'Sum and Substance' (plantain lily) (foliage)
Hypericum 'Hidcote' (St John's wort)
Malus 'Golden Hornet' (apple) (fruit)
Philadelphus coronarius 'Aureus' (mock orange) (foliage)
Phlomis fruticosa (Jerusalem sage)
Potentilla fruticosa 'Goldfinger'
Ranunculus acris 'Flore Pleno' (meadow buttercup)
Rosa 'Graham Thomas' (rose)
Sambucus racemosa 'Plumosa Aurea' (red-berried elder) (foliage)

Day lilies come in a wide range of colours.

Top ten green plants

Alchemilla mollis (lady's mantle)
Euphorbia characias subsp. *wulfenii* (spurge)
Fatsia japonica (Japanese aralia) (foliage)
Griselinia littoralis (broadleaf) (foliage)
Hosta ventricosa (plantain lily) (foliage)
Itea ilicifolia
Kniphofia 'Percy's Pride' (red hot poker)
Matteuccia struthiopteris (ostrich fern) (foliage)
Nicotiana langsdorffii (tobacco plant)
Zinnia elegans 'Envy'

Nicotiana langsdorffii *is a favourite green plant.*

Top ten purple plants

Allium aflatuense
Astrantia major 'Hadspen Blood' (Hattie's
    pincushion) (flowers and foliage)
Clematis 'Purpurea Plena Elegans'
Cotinus coggygria 'Royal Purple' (smoke bush)
Echinacea purpurea (coneflower)
Geranium phaeum var. *phaeum* 'Samobor'
Magnolia lilliflora 'Nigra'
Phormium tenax 'Purpureum' (flax)
Rosa 'Roseraie de l'Haÿ' (rose)
Sambucus nigra 'Black Lace' (black elder)
    (foliage)

There are plenty of purple varieties of allium.

Top ten blue plants

Caryopteris x *clandonensis* 'Arthur Simmonds'
Ceratostigma willmottianum
Geranium 'Johnson's Blue' (cranesbill)
Hibiscus syriacus 'Blue Bird'
Hosta sieboldiana var. *elegans* (plantain lily)
    (foliage)
Hydrangea macrophylla 'Blue Wave'
Lavandula 'Hidcote Blue' (lavender)
Nepeta 'Six Hills Giant' (catmint)
Perovskia 'Blue Spire'
Scabiosa 'Butterfly Blue' (small scabious)

*Cornflowers (*Centaurea cyanus*) are stunningly blue.*

Some colour combinations ...

Red and green are a stunning contrast in garden plantings and this is because they are opposite each other on the colour wheel, in the same way that blue is complementary to orange and yellow to violet.

The photograph left shows a red border using 'hot' coloured flowers, such as red roses and hemerocallis, which contrast not only with the green foliage immediately surrounding them, but with the yew hedge behind. The colour scheme is further reinforced by using red foliage plants, such as *Cotinus coggygria* 'Royal Purple', *Cordyline australis* 'Purpurea' and *Corylus maxima* 'Purpurea'. Other red flowers you could use include *Penstemon* 'Garnet', *Lobelia cardinalis* and *Dahlia* 'Bishop of Llandaff', all of which give the same intensity of colour.

In my garden I have used a purple-leaved cotinus in a slightly different combination, using harmonizing colours – those that are adjacent on the colour wheel – rather than complementary ones (below left). The purple foliage of *Cotinus* 'Grace' works with the soft pink petals of the herbaceous poppy (*Papaver*

orientalis species), and it is further enhanced by the blue-green foliage of *Euphorbia characias* subsp. *wulfenii* in front and behind, with yet more texture and harmony supplied by the beautiful ferny foliage of the bronze fennel (*Foeniculum vulgare* 'Purpureum').The poppy flowers for a short period in early summer so to extend the soft pink colour theme, a shrub rose such as *Rosa* 'Eglantyne' could be used.

In a dry, sun-baked area of my garden I have planted drought-resistant plants such as the grey-leaved artemisia, santolina and *Ballota pseudodictamnus* (opposite). When using silver foliage, bear in mind that most of these plants originate from arid climates so will need sunny, dry conditions. Silver foliage associates well with many other colours, such as purple foliage plants including *Pittosporum tenuifolium* 'Tom Thumb' or the evergreen perennial *Heuchera micrantha* var. *diversifolia* 'Palace Purple'. Within this area I have chosen a predominantly soft yellow colour scheme using plants such

*We all have our favourites when it comes to colour, but do experiment with different combinations. I have found that the most popular colour combinations are soft pinks, mauves and misty blues, just like the clematis and rose pictured here. The colours harmonize with each other (**right**), and give that much sought-after romantic feel.*

as *Phlomis russeliana*, *Anthemis tinctoria* 'E. C. Buxton' and fennel, which associate beautifully with the golden stems and flowers of the ornamental grass *Stipa gigantea*. For late season interest I have also planted some pale yellow hardy chrysanthemums and *Kniphofia* 'Little Maid'. By choosing pale yellows, a cooler, subdued colour scheme has been achieved giving a soft, romantic feel to this part of the garden.

There are endless colour combinations that you can experiment with in your garden. The most important thing is that it pleases your eye, as colour is such a personal choice. Remember that if you don't like a particular colour scheme you can always change it – and be open to nature taking matters into her own hands. A self-sown seedling can often upstage your best-made plans, so keep an open mind, and perhaps take photographs of successful combinations for future reference.

Good planting

When you are new to gardening, it is a little overwhelming to visit the garden centre and be confronted with a dizzying array of a few hundred different varieties of plants, when all that you need is just one plant to fill in a small space. So it's best to go having already decided what variety you are going to buy, after carefully considering your needs – I don't recommend making impulse buys!

Buying new plants

If you need to buy some new plants, ask yourself the following questions while you are at home and in your garden:

- What type of plant do I need for that empty space?
- Should it be a tree for a focal point or for 'instant' screening? (Remember to find out how large it will eventually grow.)
- Or how about a shrub? These are some of the most trouble-free plants you can buy and you get colour year after year, plus form and texture.
- Or perhaps I could use some perennial plants for an informal summer border, possibly between or in front of existing shrubs?
- Perhaps I need some climbers; for screening or training over an existing or new structure?
- Or annuals as a temporary filler for the summer? There is always a gap somewhere to fill with a few annuals.

Having identified what type of plant you need, you should then decide what function you would like the new plant to perform:

- Is it to be a focal point plant?
- Does it need to be evergreen?
- What size can it grow to?
- What colour flowers or leaves?
- Does it need to be happy in shade or sun?

If space permits, you should be planting in odd-numbered groups, and don't be afraid to repeat the same shrub in other places. This will help give your garden a sense of unity. If you have one area that needs six shrubs to fill it, don't be tempted to buy six different varieties. It is far better to select two different varieties, remembering to be aware of their form and texture, and plant three of each of them.

Choosing plants

So where should you go to buy your plants? Usually a local garden centre or nursery is the first choice as the staff there will have a good knowledge of what plants will do well in your locality. They will also be close at hand for any additional information that you may need about your purchases.

Plants may also be purchased by mail order from many excellent specialist suppliers. One of the big advantages of buying from such a grower is that the choice of varieties will be much greater. A specialist

rose grower, for instance, will have many more varieties than you will be offered in a typical garden centre. Whether you use a specialist rose, tree or herbaceous plant supplier, they will probably choose to send you plants at a time of year when they are dormant. Sometimes this means that they may not initially look quite as good as prime garden centre specimens as they will often be 'bare root' rather than potted into containers. But usually you get much better value plants, and often discounts for buying in quantity.

Remember that when you look at the prices of plants a lot of work has gone into producing that plant, and growing it on to a reasonable size. Slower growing and difficult to propagate varieties tend to be more expensive than faster growing ones.

If you are patient, you only need one plant to start you off, especially with many easy-to-grow hardy shrubs and fast spreading perennials. You can then follow my recommended techniques to propagate the plants yourself (see pages 186–9).

When you are choosing which plants to buy from a nursery ensure that they are in good condition. You don't necessarily need to buy plants that are in flower – instead look for strong growth and specimens that are well cared for.

Containers

Using containers in your garden offers an opportunity to introduce colour or foliage in areas where traditional planting would be otherwise difficult or impossible. Containers can be used to give formality to a garden design, for instance by positioning lines of pots repeating a chosen planting scheme. Or use them in an informal way by grouping together different containers with varied contents, creating a relaxed, colourful and attractive arrangement. Plenty of design ideas for each season are given on pages 144–9.

How to prepare containers

The important thing about container gardening is to prepare the pot correctly before planting, in order to give your chosen plants the best chance of successful growth (see the pictures below).

You then need to consider which type of compost or growing medium you are going to use for your plants. The choice depends on what you are planting. Walk into anywhere that is selling garden products and you will undoubtedly be deluged with a choice of composts from multi-purpose to more specific ones for Bonsai, cactus and orchid growing.

1
Start with a clean container. I would recommend that even with new containers, you take just a few minutes to scrub them thoroughly before planting to ensure that no pests or problem-causing organisms are left in the container. They could damage or harm your new plants irredeemably.

2
Ensure that free drainage of water is enhanced by placing some broken crocks over the drainage hole, or holes, in the bottom of the container. Other materials such as broken bricks will do this job just as well. Again, ensure your drainage material is thoroughly clean before putting it into the container. You may or may not choose to line the pot first with plastic (see water loss tips on page 143).

Above: Look for unusual containers for your garden: old chimney pots are quite easy to buy and are very decorative too. This one is planted with Liriope muscari, *an evergreen perennial with purple flowers in late summer. **Above right:** Be generous with your seasonal plantings; containers look best when they are overflowing with plants.*

I would always recommend that you choose peat-free compost for potting up your containers. More than 94 per cent of peat bogs in Britain have been destroyed or damaged, and once destroyed they are gone for ever. Peat bog areas are among the most important of wildlife habitats and because amateur gardeners buy composts containing peat, they account for about 70 per cent of peat use. Peat is formed over very long periods by the decomposition of plant materials and it is used in compost to help retain moisture as well as supply minerals essential for growth. But, it also easily becomes waterlogged or can dry out completely and then be difficult to wet again. The good news is that there is an increasing choice of peat-free composts available and here are the main ones.

Loam-based potting composts: These are essentially sterilized garden soil with added nutrients. Some loam based composts contain a percentage of peat so please be careful to study the composition of the compost and choose one with a peat substitute content. These composts are generally good for healthy root growth and even though

> Loamless composts can be difficult to re-wet if they have been allowed to dry out too much. To help avoid this, buy wetting agents from your local garden centre. These mainly take the form of granules or crystals that you mix with the compost. When the compost is watered, these granules expand to form a gel that is moisture retentive and so the compost will lose less water.

Drainage pipes may be bought cheaply at builders' yards and make great containers for these alpines.

they drain well, they dry out more slowly than loamless composts. Use a loam-based compost if you are intending to plant long-lived plants or shrubs.

Loamless potting composts: These are the most common type of potting composts, but many are peat-based, so look out for ones that use peat substitutes. Loamless potting composts tend to be more open in their stucture and are good for seasonal plantings, such as summer bedding plants. Composts are usually sold as multi-purpose, so you can use them for seed sowing, taking cuttings or potting up plants.

Coir: Coir is increasingly used as a peat substitute and even though it dries more slowly than peat, I have found that mixing it with organic compost, such as leaf mould (see page 165), helps moisture retention. It also gives more body to the compost and in this way provides a healthy growing medium for your plants.

Organic matter: I like to add some garden compost or other organic matter as well. Organic matter holds moisture like a sponge and releases it as the surrounding soil becomes dry (see page 177).

Remember that containers need not only be used for seasonal plantings, there are many long-lived plants and shrubs that you can use for a more permanent planting scheme in your garden. The use of long-lived plants and shrubs in containers is less common than seasonal displays. They need more care and attention in order to help them with regards to moisture retention and essential nutrient feeds. However, the extra effort is well worth it and will reward you with a long-term planting scheme that can be used very effectively to provide dramatic focus and maturity.

How to feed container-grown plants

A valuable asset for container-grown plants is slow-release nutrient plugs. These are readily available at your garden centre and they ensure a slow, even release of fertilizer into the compost, providing essential nutrients for your plants. However, nothing can compensate for keeping a close eye on your plants to know that they are vibrant and in good health, so an application of soluble or diluted liquid feed may also be required from time to time.

How to slow down water loss from containers

1
Unlike glazed or plastic pots, terracotta and wood are porous materials so are prone to losing moisture. Line them with plastic, but don't forget to make some drainage holes at the bottom.

2
Dark containers absorb more heat than light coloured ones. I've painted some of mine in pretty pastel shades, which is also a simple and effective way of adding some colour into the garden.

3
Always mulch containers to help reduce moisture loss. Gravel, pebbles, glass beads, shells or bark chippings are just a few of the many mulches available from garden centres. Why not put a use to all your used bottle corks? They'll bring back happy memories every time you look at them.

4
An informal group of containers placed together makes them easier to water.

Spring containers

The first flowers of spring are a welcome sight after winter. There are many spring-flowering bulbs and other colourful plants that can be used for a spring display. There is such a good range of plants at most garden centres that it is still possible to buy flowering bulbs and plants in the spring for some instant colour. However, traditionally spring-flowering containers are planted up in the autumn, which is bulb planting time, and spring-flowering bedding plants such as wallflowers are also for sale. Daffodils, tulips, crocus, hyacinths and muscari are some of the best bulbs for spring containers.

Above: A hanging basket romantically planted with wallflowers, violas, hyacinths and Ranunculus asiaticus. *Right:* A more formal planting of white violas and Erysimum *'Bowles' Mauve'.*

Spring-flowering plants for containers

Crocuses
Dwarf daffodils
Erysimum (wallflowers)
Hyacinths
Myosotis (forget-me-nots)
Pansies and violas
Polyanthus and primroses
Ranunculus asiaticus
Tulips

When selecting daffodils, choose the smaller varieties as the full-size daffodils will look too large for most plantings. Tulips come in a huge range of colours and sizes, and if you have room, it's possible to plant early and late flowering varieties in the same container to prolong the flowering period.

Choosing a container

When you make your selection for planting up, there are many different styles you can aim for. A contemporary metal container would call for a bold planting of a single colour of wallflowers, possibly underplanted with a single colour of tulips, while a country style basket would suit a more romantic planting; a mixture of fragrant pink hyacinths, blue and yellow violas, pink ranunculus and creamy-yellow sweetly scented wallflowers. With many of these spring-flowering bulbs and flowers coming in such a range of colours, the colour combinations and styles you can create are endless.

How to create a simple country-style planting

I love seeing wild daffodils flowering in farmland in the spring, and this simple container planting echoes that – all that is missing are the lambs! Fill the container in the autumn, and by the spring you will get daffodils growing naturally through the grass. After they have finished flowering, transplant them to a permanent position in grass or in a border in the garden, where they will continue to flower year after year. I chose to use a variety of daffodil called 'Tête-à-Tête' – although it isn't a true wild daffodil, it looks similar.

KIM'S TIP

> Wherever possible, plant containers in the position they are to be sited as, once filled, a container can often be very heavy. This makes it more difficult to move it to your chosen location and increases the risk of damage to your plants and, of course, injury to yourself.

1
Select a simple, small window box, and prepare it as described on page 140. From a garden centre buy a variety of dwarf daffodil called 'Tête-à-Tête'. Part fill with compost and space your bulbs throughout the container 10cm (4in) apart, with the pointed end upwards.

2
Cut thin hazel sticks and insert them around the edge of the container. Tie on some horizontal sticks using twine to create a rustic, rail fence effect. Fill with more compost and top with turf. Water well and then await the spring.

Summer containers

For many people, summer-flowering containers are the most important. They give an endless succession of flowers in the warmer months when we are using our gardens the most. More tender varieties of plants may be used, which therefore gives a huge choice of planting possibilities.

During the warm summer weather, watering your containers is really important. Plants that are allowed to dry out too much will often cease flowering for a while, and can develop burnt edges to their leaves. Feeding is essential, too; most potting composts have enough nutrients added to them to keep your container plants well fed for six to eight weeks. After this a liquid feed added to the watering will maintain healthy growth and a succession of flowers for as long as possible.

After selecting your flowering plants, consider using a few taller growing varieties for some extra height and contrast. Cannas, *Abutilon* x *hybridum*, *Amaranthus caudatus*, brugmansias and purple millet (*Pennisetum glaucum* 'Purple Majesty') can all be used to excellent and dramatic effect in summer container plantings.

Summer-flowering plants for containers

Dwarf dahlia	Pelargonium
Fuchsia	Petunias
Heliotrope	*Salvia* (sage)
Impatiens (busy Lizzie)	Tagetes (marigolds)
Lobelia	Verbena

Left: *Contemporary containers look good with dramatic foliage such as this purple millet (*Pennisetum glaucum *'Purple Majesty') and the contrasting colours of deep red petunias and verbenas with white impatiens.* **Opposite:** *The style of your container will dictate your choice of plants, whether they be frothy and romantic for terracotta or more delineated for stainless steel. Don't forget summer climbers. I've made wigwams of willow stems for sweet pea seedlings to grow up.*

Winter containers

Through the cold months of winter there are still some attractive plants that can be used in containers. Evergreen foliage becomes much more important in the winter and there is a variety of colourful foliage available. Common ivy, for example, has many different forms, some with colourful yellow or white variegated foliage and all varieties look good planted at the edges of containers for a trailing effect. For an extra splash of late winter colour, plant a few small bulbs like crocus around the edges. At Christmas, why not push red-berried holly stems into the planting, or use bright red ribbons or string tied around the containers for some extra festive decoration?

Evergreens for winter containers

Calluna vulgaris varieties
Cordyline australis 'Purpurea'
Euonymus fortunei 'Emerald Gaiety'
Heuchera varieties
Mahonia aquifolium 'Apollo'
Ornamental cabbage and kale
Pieris japonica

Viburnum tinus is an especially good winter plant, it has heads of flowers that are deep pink in bud, opening white, and may also have bluish purple berries at the same time. *Skimmia japonica* performs in a similar way with attractive flower buds, flowers and berries all set against glossy green foliage. Both plants would look great as a simple mass planting in a large container.

Remember, too, that a container itself can add some colour in winter. Terracotta is a warm pinkish-red more noticeable in winter against foliage colours. There are also many glazed pots with various colours, but choose carefully so that it complements your chosen plantings rather than becoming too dominant.

Winter containers can be a colourful mixture of seasonal flowers or, for a more contemporary look, try a single evergreen plant that has a strong form to it.

How to plant a colourful pot for extra winter colour

Here is a colourful glazed pot used as the basis for a simple midwinter planting.

KIM'S TIP

> As we tend to
> use our gardens
> less in winter,
> it's worth
> creating winter
> container
> plantings that
> will be easily
> seen from
> inside the
> house.

1
Prepare the pot as described on page 140. When selecting the plants, I decided to keep the arrangement simple and chose flower and foliage colours to harmonize with the colours of the pot. The *Mahonia aquifolium* 'Apollo' has marvellous bright yellow flowers in keeping with the top of the pot's glaze.

2
Plant the focal point in the centre of the pot to give height and structure. To complement the mahonia I also selected the evergreen sedge, *Uncinia rubra*, for its dramatic foliage colour, which toned with the container. It also provided a splendid contrast in texture and form.

3
Plant each of the surrounding plants evenly around the edge of the pot, ensuring they drape casually over the container's rim.

Part 5
GARDEN TECHNIQUES

I remember the first seeds I sowed were in my newly made raised vegetable beds, and I was amazed that a plant could grow from such tiny beginnings. Growing vegetables was the first thing that got me outside and growing plants, and watching my children enjoying the first carrots that I'd ever sown was a fabulous feeling. Whether you're growing vegetables for the first time, sowing seeds, taking cuttings or planting a tree, you'll quickly gain confidence and discover just how enjoyable it is to be out in the garden and learning new skills.

First things first

You may find that like many new gardeners you have acquired several garden tools, from family, friends or 'found in the shed' when you moved to your present home. But what tools do you really need for your garden, and how do you use them correctly? The tools that you need will depend on what type of garden you have. A larger garden with trees, hedges and vegetables will require a greater variety of tools than a small urban space. Identifying what tasks you will be doing in your garden will help you decide which tools you will need to invest in. There are two main types of garden tools: powered tools and hand tools.

Power tools

In a small garden with a lawn, the main powered tool you are likely to need is a lawnmower. The size and type should be dictated by the size of your lawn. Petrol mowers are better for larger areas, although this means having to buy and store fuel, and maintain the engine. Electric mowers are much easier for small lawns, but using one that is too small for your lawn will increase the time spent on grass cutting.

It is probably cheaper to hire any other power tools you may find you only occasionally need. For example, you may only need to use hedge trimmers or a Rotovator to turn over soil once or twice a year. When using any power tools, make sure to follow all the manufacturer's recommended safety instructions.

Ten essential garden hand tools

Digging fork
Digging spade
Hoe
Lawn/leaf rake
Secateurs
Shears
Soil rake
Trowel
Weeding bucket
Wheelbarrow

Hand tools

A list of essential hand tools is given on the left. Other hand tools you may need include long-handled edging shears for the lawn edges, long-handled pruners and a pruning saw. Gardening gloves, a watering can, a hosepipe and a good broom are useful additions too.

When selecting new tools, choose ones that are comfortable to grip and hold. With digging forks and spades it's also important that the handles are long enough so as not to put strain on the back. It is worth spending more money on more expensive tools, which may be easier to use and ultimately last longer than their cheaper counterparts.

Look after your hand tools by always cleaning them after each use. Before putting them away, scrub off any soil with water and rub dry with an oily rag. Store all tools neatly out of children's way, preferably under lock and key.

Organizing your shed

Generally, I think you can't have a shed that's too big; the larger it is, the easier it will be to organize. To make the most of what space you have, you will need shelves, and lots of them! It's really just like organizing a kitchen – think about which items will need to be stored and the most space-saving way to do this.

Hang up as many items as possible: Most garden tools can be hung on hooks or nails, saving space and also preventing potential accidents. Make sure you have hooks next to the tools for a stiff hand brush and an oiled rag, for cleaning the tools each time they are put away. This is an essential part of maintaing your tools and is a habit it is well worth getting into.

A well-organized shed is essential and I'm pleased to say that this tidy shed is my own!

Other handy storage devices: Many DIY stores sell useful storage products. A mechanic's tool box, for example, is an excellent way to store small items such as secateurs, string, ties, hand tools and plant labels. Also large, clear glass jars, recycled from the kitchen, are handy; they can hold smaller items such as nails and screws, all neatly arranged on a shelf without the need for labels.

The hosepipe: Make sure you buy a hosepipe reel, not only does it store the hosepipe well, it also reduces wear and tear on the pipe itself. Portable ones are available, and the best ones have a 'flow through' design, enabling the hose to be used without unwinding the whole length.

An occasional good sort-out of your shed is not a bad idea either. Seek advice from your local authority for any old garden chemicals that you may find; they will arrange for their safe disposal. Bags of potting compost will not keep indefinitely as the added nutrients only last for a limited time, so use up any old potting compost as a soil conditioner.

Finally, remember that by having an organized storage space you will have more time to work in and enjoy your garden!

Organic gardening

Organic gardening is gardening with nature – being kind to the environment and kind to humans too. Organic practices aren't just for vegetable growers, they can be applied to all areas of a garden without you having to completely convert to *The Good Life*! You just have to look and see how much organic food is now available in supermarkets to realise that the 'organic' way is proving irresistible to people who have grown suspicious of chemical and pesticide scares, BSE (mad cow disease) and genetic modification (GM). People want to know their health and that of their children is as protected as can be. The cumulative effect of pesticides we consume in our everyday food is very worrying, so it's not surprising that people are 'going organic'.

Everyone loves to see butterflies in their garden, and Verbena bonariensis *is one of the many flowers that will attract them.*

Environmental pollution has, of course, taken a heavy toll on wildlife and the environment, with species becoming threatened or extinct, rivers polluted and warnings of global warming caused by CO_2 emissions due to the burning of fossil fuels and deforestation. Some people argue that climate change has occurred many times in the earth's history so there's nothing to worry about; indeed, it is true that our current warming has been occurring for the last 150 years, but what is so alarming is the speed at which the present warming is happening. In climate terms, the average temperature is rising so fast in Britain that gardens are moving south at the rate of 12m (13yd) a day! It is clearly time for all of us to contribute to a healthier world in any way we can, and remember that we do not inherit this world from our ancestors, but borrow it from our children.

Top ten organic tips

1. **Healthy plants thrive in healthy soil.** Improve the quality of your soil by adding plenty of organic matter such as compost, leaf mould or well-rotted manure (see page 30).

2. **Encourage wildlife to help control pests** (see pages 156–8). Use organic insecticides and fungicides only as a last measure.

3. **Make your planting as diverse as possible.** Scientists have found that habitats containing a greater variety of species are healthier and more stable.

4. **Wise up to water.** On a global scale, water is a scarce and precious resource and domestic use accounts for 65 per cent of the total water used by humanity.

Water is also expensive, especially if metered, so try the following ideas:

- Choose plants to suit your soil, aspect and climate and incorporate organic matter into the soil to help retain moisture.
- Collect rainwater in water butts.
- Only water in the evening when the air and soil are cool so less water will be lost through evaporation, and always direct water at the plant roots rather than on the plant itself.
- Avoid sprinklers as most of the water is blown away, but where watering is essential, consider laying down hose with tiny holes running along it.

5 **Weeds.** Plant densely, not only does it look good, but it inhibits weeds from getting a look in. Use mulches either by planting groundcover plants, which make a living mulch, look good and retain moisture in the soil, or use loose mulches such as bark chippings, leaf mould or gravel.

- Loose mulches need to be 10cm (4in) deep on soil that has already had all weeds cleared and had a good soaking. Apply in spring when the soil warms up (see also page 177). For further weed prevention, put down a layer of permeable membrane before adding the mulch.
- Use a hoe in the borders to dislodge weeds; hand weeding is easier after a rainy day. For large areas that need to be cleared of weeds, use a light excluding membrane, such as black polythene

sheeting, but allow water and air into the soil after two months.

- Use geotextile membrane under gravel or patio areas to minimize weeds, and consider pointing paving with mortar rather than filling with sand.

6 **Choose any timber products** from well-managed, sustainable sources. Look out for wood with the Forest Stewardship Council (FSC) label on. Re-use and recycle where possible and use local resources, which will cut down on pollution caused by transport.

7 **Choose peat-free composts.** Peat bogs have taken 10,000 years to form and once destroyed are gone forever. More than 94 per cent of lowland bogs in Britain have been destroyed. Peat-free composts are available from any garden centre (see also pages 141–2).

8 **Make your own garden compost** by recycling kitchen and garden waste (see pages 162–5).

9 **Plant a tree.** One of the greatest pleasures of planting for me is to plant a tree. Not only do they clean the air we breathe but they provide food and shelter for wildlife while providing structure, height and beauty in the garden (see pages 172–3).

10 **Join Garden Organic (formerly the HDRA).** This is one of the world's foremost authorities on organic gardening, and you can phone their helpline if you have a query. Very handy!

How to plant through a membrane

1
Scrape back the mulch to reveal as much membrane as you need to dig through.

2
Use a sharp knife or scissors to cut a cross through the membrane and then peel back the material.

3
Dig an appropriate-sized hole, transferring all soil to a container. Plant as usual (see page 171), fold down the membrane and re-cover with the mulch.

Controlling pests and diseases

For me one of the great pleasures of being outside in my garden is seeing and hearing the local wildlife, from the elegant swoop of a swallow, to the hoot of an owl when I take our dog for a late night stroll. Wildlife is increasingly at risk, with natural habitats being threatened by encroaching urbanization and industrialized farming practices. But, thankfully, us humble gardeners don't have to take this lying down!

Both the young larvae and the adult ladybird beetles have a huge appetite for greenfly, and should be welcomed into any garden.

Our gardens can easily provide alternative habitats for wildlife, while at the same time promoting a natural balance in the garden where plants and wildlife co-exist and flourish. Children love digging for worms, chasing butterflies and watching as a ladybird scuttles across their fingers, so wildlife gardens are perfect for them too. What is a garden without the sweet song of a robin or blackbird, the drowsy hum of bees, or the air acrobatics of a dragonfly? These are the moments I treasure in our garden, so I find there is a strong motivation to plant a diverse range of plants. To encourage many forms of wildlife to take up residence, it is also important to create shelter and provide water.

Gardening and having children began at about the same time for me, and from day one it has always been a priority to grow things organically to keep the garden healthy and safe for all garden dwellers without the use of pesticides, insecticides and other chemicals. Apart from any environmental or health issues, applying chemicals is a real bore, and storing them always potentially hazardous. Organic gardening puts emphasis on healthy soil = healthy plants = healthy environment! Just like us humans, healthy plants are better equipped to tolerate pests and diseases than unhealthy ones.

Keeping your plants healthy

Look to see if your soil is in good condition (see pages 26–9). If necessary, improve its quality with the addition of good garden compost (see page 30) to encourage strong healthy growth. Healthy plants are more disease immune than unhealthy ones.

Remember: right plant, right place: A sun-loving plant will only sulk or die in a shady spot; likewise, a plant that prefers damp conditions will not be at its best in a sunny place. Read the labels, ask questions at the garden centre and look up the plant's requirements.

Keep planting diverse: Research has shown that mixed planting can cut down on plant damage by pests. Growing only one kind of plant (a monoculture), for example roses, can create conditions where pests and diseases will thrive.

Encourage beneficial insects into the garden such as ladybirds, hoverflies and lacewings, which devour aphids.

Encourage birds such as thrushes and blackbirds into the garden to devour slugs and snails, as well as delight you with bird song.

Plants that attract beneficial insects

Calendula officinalis (marigolds)
Centranthus ruber (valerian)
Daisies
Foeniculum vulgare (fennel)
Hedera (ivy)
Lavandula (lavender)
Limnanthes douglasii (poached egg flower)
Mentha (mint)
Papaver (poppies)
Rosa canina (dog rose)

*Mixed plantings (**below right**) are the key to maintaining a population of beneficial insects, which, in turn, will help keep pests under control. Calendulas (**below**) are one of the bright daisy-shaped flowers that attract hoverflies, which then prey on aphids, and a lavender plant in flower (**bottom**) will attract hundreds of bees into your garden. Bees pollinate many of your plants as they fly from flower to flower collecting nectar.*

KIM'S TIPS

> While the use of Glyphosate cannot be recommended for organic gardeners, its wide use deserves a mention here. Glyphosate products such as Roundup are non-selective herbicides – they are poisonous to all plants and so are very effective weed killers.

> Although the active ingredients are rapidly broken down on contact with soil, recent research suggests that Roundup kills frogs and tadpoles in very low concentrations, as well as upsetting the fragile ecological balance in the garden.

> Try to take all the steps you can to avoid resorting to chemicals anywhere in the garden.

Scare unwanted birds from the vegetable patch or where new seed has been sown by erecting a washing line of old CDs, which will glint in the sun (funnily enough, I've found a number of my own recordings to be extremely effective!).

Attract a wide range of wildlife: A good way to do this is by creating a permanent log pile. Leaving dead wood in the garden is hugely beneficial to a wide range of wildlife, especially beetles, hedgehogs, frogs and toads, who will go to work on slugs and snails for you.

Kill slugs and snails: Slug pellets don't just kill slugs, they kill the animals that eat them too and should be avoided.

- Environmentally safe alternatives include beer traps, which can be sunk into the ground with the lip raised 2–3cm ($^3/_4$–1$^1/_4$in) above the soil.
- Over-turned grapefruit skins provide a moist refuge during the day – offenders can be dealt with in any way you see fit! (Dropping them in salt water will finish them off if you can't bring yourself to.)
- Sharp sand, soot, eggshells and coffee grounds are all recommended, too, but with varying results. It might be better instead to plant all susceptible plants like hostas in containers with vaseline smeared around the rim. Copper tape is also available that emits a tiny electric charge that soon has a slug on the run.
- It is also worth remembering that slugs can't swim, so by creating a little moat made from plastic guttering around a raised bed, you will ensure they leave empty-handed.
- Protect vulnerable new plants such as seedlings, annuals or herbaceous plants with plastic bottle cloches with lids left off.

Kill greenfly: An aphid infestation (left) is easy to dislodge from plants with a short, sharp blast of water from the hose. Spraying with a dilute mix of water and washing-up liquid will also do the trick. Better though to encourage natural predators such as ladybirds, lacewings and hoverflies (see above).

Kill vine weevils: Plants in pots are particularly vulnerable to these destructive pests whose larvae feed on root plants. The first you'll know about it is when the plant suddenly wilts and dies, while adults eat irregular holes around the edges of leaves.

- Protect individual pots by using sticky tape smeared with non-drying glue (vine weevils can't fly).

Roses: common problems

Fungal diseases such as blackspot and powdery mildew are the bane of rose lovers everywhere.

Black spots appear on leaves and stems of roses in early summer after having overwintered on the plant, or on infected fallen leaves.

Powdery mildew is an off-white powdery, fungal growth, which also overwinters on the plant in the same way.

Both diseases cause defoliation and weaken the rose. To help prevent these problems, choose old rose varieties, many of which have natural disease resistance. Look for 'Charles de Mills', 'Comte de Chambord' and 'Gertrude Jekyll'. Disease-resistant roses include all the *Rugosa* roses such as 'Fru Dagmar Hastrup' (pink), 'Roseraie de l'Haÿ' (purple) and 'Blanche Double de Coubert' (white), as well as species roses such as *R. glauca*, grown for its purple foliage and long lasting red hips, *R.* 'Geranium' with brilliant red flowers and large hips, and *R. xanthina* 'Canary Bird', with single yellow flowers.

If disaster strikes: Remove all infected and fallen leaves as soon as you see them and burn them. Whatever else you do, don't put them on the compost heap or the disease will spread. Prune roses in the spring so they have a good open shape (see page 184) and air can move around more freely. Also spray with an organic fungicide available from Garden Organic (formely known as the Henry Doubleday Research Assocation, or the HDRA). Mulching in late winter will help to smother any fungal spores overwintering on fallen leaves. Mulching will also conserve moisture in the soil and suppress weeds, especially if it is applied in spring when the earth has started to warm up.

Roses are one of the most popular of garden plants. If you keep having fungal problems with your roses (the leaves to the left show what mildew looks like), it may be best to replant them with a more resistant variety, such as Rosa rugosa (**above left**). *It's best to always plant roses in a fresh area of ground where they have not been grown before. Specialist rose suppliers will be happy to give you plenty of advice on choosing suitable varieties.*

Forking and digging

The soil in your garden may need cultivating for severeral different reasons. You may need to clear an area of perennial weeds, incorporate extra organic matter or prepare an area for seed sowing. The task that you are going to do dictates whether you need to use a fork or spade.

Use a digging fork to remove perennial weeds from beds and borders. A spade would chop through the roots and any roots left behind would regrow, whereas the fork will help you to lift the whole of the weed out of the soil easily.

In my garden I carry out two types of digging: new areas of garden or borders that need some rejuvenation require more intensive digging, while a light forking over of the soil is all that I do just once a year for established borders. The two main tools in any digging task are, of course, the fork and the spade.

Forking over soil

The fork is mainly used to turn over borders and beds in previously cultivated areas in preparation for a new growing season. This allows you to break up any large clods of soil and remove any weeds as you go. It is not necessary to use the whole depth of the fork. The incorporation of well-rotted organic material, such as compost or leaf mould (see pages 162–5), can also be carried out at this stage (or when digging, see opposite) and will progressively improve soil condition, leading to better growing conditions for your plants.

Digging over soil

The spade is for more serious digging and is generally used in areas that need to be prepared for new planting or for cultivation of vegetables. When turning over soil, always dig to the depth of the blade and in regular trenches, working steadily and methodically

When you use a spade to dig, you turn over greater volumes of soil than with a fork. This makes a spade more suitable to use if you want to incorporate organic matter into the soil.

from one side of the plot to the other. By working in this way you will ensure that you cover every bit of the ground. Start by digging a trench at the furthermost end of the bed. Put the soil you dig from this trench to one side. Then dig the next trench, turning over the soil and putting it into the first trench. Continue to work in this way, until you reach the end of the plot. Use a wheelbarrow to bring the soil from the first trench you dug to fill the final trench.

Add organic matter: If your soil is poor, this is the time to add organic material in the form of compost or leaf mould (see pages 162–5). Simply add the organic material to the bottom of each trench as you dig. This will improve the structure, moisture retention and soil fertility, leading to better results from the plants.

Good techniques

Once you have finished forking or digging, avoid standing on the area. Walking on newly cultivated soil compacts the soil structure, making it more difficult for the plants' roots to grow.

To avoid possible aches and pains, make sure you have a good quality fork or spade that is a comfortable weight and size. Also, don't attempt to dig too large an area at once, take regular breaks and change to a different task for a while. If you have a large area to be dug over, consider hiring a Rotovator. They are easy to use and tool hire companies will show you how to handle them safely and properly.

Composting

Making your own garden compost is an easy way to help the environment and your garden. Garden compost is decomposed organic matter produced by bacteria breaking down certain garden and household waste. It is excellent for enriching your garden soil, and the more you enrich and improve your garden soil, the healthier and happier your plants will be.

Composting is easy with just a few simple guidelines to follow. A compost heap is the simplest arrangement, but a bin will do just as well. The compost heap initially heats up as bacteria and micro-organisms get to work on the waste matter. Then it cools down and worms and other beneficial insects break down the material even more.

A medium-sized compost heap can heat up to 70°C (158°F) in a few days. The heat helps to make compost more quickly, and to kill weeds and diseases. Your compost may not heat up this much, but it will be just as good. It will just take longer before it's ready for use.

Positioning your compost bin

A compost bin is not essential, but I prefer to use one as it keeps everything neater. So the first thing to do is to buy or make a compost bin and decide where to put it. Site it in a sunny place if possible as warmth from the sun also helps to speed up the composting process. It needs to be open to soil underneath to encourage earth worms to be involved in the process.

How to make a composter

Well, you should be convinced by now of the merits of composting your garden and household waste, so here's a quick and easy way to make your own compost bin. We asked a local store for some wooden pallets that they were throwing away, and with some timber posts and a few nails had built a new compost bin in minutes!

First, carefully choose the best place for your compost bin, remembering that a sunny spot is better if possible. Level the site and remove any

1
Gather together your materials close to where you will build your composter.

2
The first pallet forms the back of the compost bin. Hold it in place and put one of the posts down through the gap in the middle of the pallet.

3
Hold the post against the inside corner of the pallet and, using the lump hammer, drive the post into the ground. Nail the pallet to the post. Take a second post and fix it in the same way at the other end of the pallet.

4
Take a second pallet, which will form one side of the compost bin, place it at a right angle to the first pallet, and then nail together the two ends.

5
Take another post, place it through the gap in the pallet at the front of the compost bin, and then drive it into the ground using the lump hammer as before. Nail the pallet to the post to secure it.

6
You will now have two sides of the bin securely fixed in place. Following the same procedure, fix the next pallet in place to form the third side.

perennial weeds if necessary. Once you've made this composter, you will have a sturdy, open-fronted compost bin, ready to use! Start filling with materials for composting and remember to lay a square of carpet on the top of the heap, to keep the rain out and the heat and moisture in.

Filling the bin

Now you have your compost bin it's time to start filling it. Just add layers of waste material as you produce them, remembering to replace the carpet lid each time. Anything that will rot will compost, but some items are best avoided. Grass mowings and soft young weeds rot down quickly, tougher plant material is slower to rot but gives more bulk to the finished compost. For best results, use a mixture of different types of waste.

Soft weeds and prunings will quickly decompose on your compost heap. I find it useful to have a trug handy in the garden to collect weeds that I pull as I walk around, or for any helpful visitors to do the same!

The main ingredients in our compost heap are:

- Weeds, small ones from hand weeding and only the tops of perennial weeds like nettles (always chop off the roots).
- Grass cuttings, including long grass when we have been strimming. I make sure the grass cuttings are mixed in with the rest of the contents because if there are a lot of them, they can create a slimy mess.
- Wood ash, from cleaning out the fireplace.
- Fruit and vegetable scraps from the kitchen, but not cooked food as that attracts mice.
- Cardboard, including egg boxes and loo roll middles. Glossy paper will not compost well so it is best to recycle.
- Young hedge clippings, plant prunings and vegetable plant remains – again, keeping as many roots out of the composter as possible.

Items not to compost are:

- Meat and fish waste
- Newspapers and glossy magazines
- Cooked food
- Coal fire ash
- Dog and cat waste
- Woody materials.

Fruit and vegetable scraps are just some of the items you can fling onto your composter.

To speed up your composting

- Chop or shred very tough stems, such as cabbage stalks, before adding them.
- With a digging fork, turn the heap over occasionally.
- Remember to keep its carpet lid on to keep in the heat.

Compost can be made in two months, or it can take a year or more. When the ingredients you have put in your container have turned into a crumbly dark brown material, the composting process is complete.

Leaf mould

Leaf mould is really easy to make using all the fallen leaves you clear up in autumn. Don't use evergreen leaves as these take too long to break down. Place damp leaves into a dustbin liner, make a few air holes, tie loosely and leave for 12 months to decay.

Leaf mould produces a rich, dark material that can be used to improve the quality of your soil at any time of year. Leaf mould can also help in the battle against weeds if placed on the surface of the soil about 10cm (4in) thick. Do this in spring when the soil starts to warm up, and as well as inhibiting unwanted weeds, it will help keep valuable moisture in the soil.

Sowing seeds outdoors

One of the cheapest and easiest ways of getting some new plants is by buying a packet of seeds and sowing them directly outdoors where they are to flower.

The types of plants that are generally grown from seed are called hardy annuals. Hardy refers to the fact that they will withstand the climate sufficiently well for direct sowing outside in the spring. Annuals are plants that grow, flower and die during one growing season. Although they need to be replaced each year, they have several advantages:

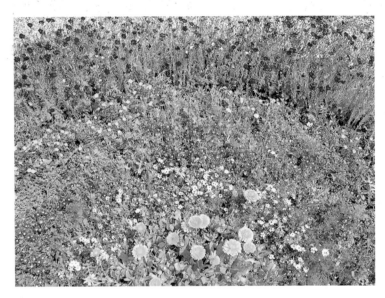

When your hardy annuals are in full flower, make sure you take some photographs to help you plan next year's display. When they have finished at the end of the year, pull up the plants and add them to the compost bin. In this lovely combination there are scarlet flax (Linum), English marigolds (Calendula officinalis), marjoram (Origanum vulgare), Legousia 'Blue Carpet' and swan river daisy (Brachyscome iberidifolia).

- A packet of hardy annual seeds is cheap, and hundreds of plants can be grown from a single packet!
- Annual flowers are very decorative and can provide great cut flowers.
- You can change your planting schemes every year.
- A new garden can have many gaps filled quickly and easily.
- They are great for getting children interested in the garden. They are easy, colourful and fast growing.
- Many annuals 'self-seed', which means they drop their own seeds that then grow and flower the following year.

Easy annual flowers

Calendula (English marigold)
Centaurea cyanus (cornflower)
Echium vulgare (viper's bugloss)
Helianthus annus (sunflower)
Iberis (candytuft)
Lathyrus (sweet pea)
Limnanthes douglasii (poached egg plant)
Nigella (love-in-a-mist)
Papaver somniferum (opium poppy)
Tropaeolum (nasturtium)
Salvia horminum (clary)

How to sow hardy annual flowers or vegetables

1
Carefully dig over the soil, removing any weeds by hand. Use a digging fork to do this so the weeds are easier to remove. Scatter a little organic granular fertilizer over the surface to give the annuals an extra feed and then use a soil rake to break down the lumps and leave a crumbly, fine surface.

2
Vegetable seeds are usually sown in rows – annuals can be too, but it is more usual to sow them in a more informal way. Use the end of the rake or hoe and draw shallow drills in your prepared seedbed. Sowing in rows makes it much easier to identify the seedlings among any weeds that may also germinate, which need to be removed. Sprinkle the seeds, if they are small, or for larger ones use your fingers, following the packet instructions for depth and spacing.

3
Carefully cover the seeds with soil using the rake or a trowel. Do not cover too deeply – in nature, most seeds drop onto the surface and just fall into shallow cracks before germinating. Label the end of the rows of the area, so you remember what you have sown! Make sure you water the seedbed after sowing and again in dry weather.

4
Vegetable and flower seedlings grow best when lightly thinned out. Removing some of the weaker seedlings will give the remaining ones more room to grow.

KIM'S TIPS

> You can tell when the soil is warm enough to sow hardy annual seeds, as weed seedlings will have started to appear.
> Annuals are a great way to attract wildlife into the garden. Flowers provide nectar for pollinating bees and insects, while seed heads provide food for birds.

Sowing seeds indoors

Nature's biggest way of plant propagation is, of course, through seeds. Although we can put to use self-sown seedlings that appear in our gardens and we can also sow seeds directly outdoors, sometimes there is an advantage to sowing seeds indoors.

You do not need a greenhouse for this, although it's a great help, but a porch or a sunny windowsill is a brilliant place to start off some seedlings. The most important factor is to have as much natural light as possible. If plants are indoors but do not have enough light, they become 'leggy' and 'drawn' and generally unhealthy.

The big advantage to sowing indoors means no frost and some extra heat, so in spring you can start off a few courgette plants two or three weeks before outdoor sowings. In turn, this will result in earlier crops. Some vegetables and flowers are not fully hardy and are slow to start in a cool spring: zinnias, courgettes, sunflowers and tomatoes all benefit from an indoor early sowing. As the seedlings emerge and then start turning into small vegetable plants you can enjoy being a part of the event.

How to grow seedlings

1
Read the instructions on your seed packet. Sow large seeds such as courgettes or sunflowers individually in small pots, using a peat-free seed-sowing compost. Use seed compost rather than potting compost as the added nutrients in potting compost are too strong for tiny seedlings.

2
Large seeds are easy to handle – simply make a hole with a pencil and drop in each seed. For smaller seeds, such as tomatoes, still use a small pot but sow a pinch of seeds onto the surface of the compost.

3
Sprinkle a little more compost on the top and water carefully. Keep moist and within a week you should see signs of growth. If the pots are on the kitchen windowsill, they can be watched on a daily basis.

Pricking out

With a single seed in each pot you can grow the seedlings on and then plant out when they are large enough. But if you have several seedlings in each pot you will need to separate them into individual pots; this is called 'pricking out'. Gently tip the seedlings out of the pot and use a plant label to ease the seedling out of the compost. Carefully separate and then in a new pot of fresh compost make a little hole and drop in the seedling's root. Slightly firm the compost around the seedling. Water and keep out of direct sunlight for a day or two.

Planting out

Whether you are growing courgettes or sunflowers, there will be a time when they really need to be planted out. This is when they have filled their pot with roots, and the weather outside should now be warm enough for your cherished new plants to be planted out. Be careful not to keep them too long in their pots. If they are left too long, they may begin to become stunted, and should be planted out without delay. They are best planted out during calm, damp weather.

How to plant out your seedlings

1
In late spring after the frosts, place your seedlings outside for a few hours each day to prepare them for being planted in the garden. This is called hardening off. If planting in the ground, remove large stones and weeds and rake until the surface is even. Dig a small hole for your first seedling.

2
Water the plants before gently tipping them out of their containers. Tap the bottom of the pot if they don't want to budge. Plant in the ground at the same level they were in the pot. Carefully firm in the soil around the plant.

3
Water again. Consider if your plant might need some support (it will tell you on the packet). Tall sunflowers can be loosely tied to a bamboo pole and climbing runner beans can be grown up a wigwam of bamboo poles. Grow peas through twiggy branches or netting.

Planting annuals, perennials and shrubs

Container-grown plants can be planted at any time of the year, except when the soil is frozen or waterlogged. Usually, perennials are bought at the start of their growing season, often when they are in flower. Although shrubs may also be bought and planted at any time, autumn planting is slightly more preferable as the shrubs establish themselves before winter and then require less summer watering in their first growing season.

When selecting your new plants, remember that it's best to limit your choice to a few different species planted in odd-numbered groups, rather than one of each of many different species. This will give far greater impact to your finished planting.

Whatever you are planting, the same principles apply (see opposite) and your aim is to make your acquisitions as comfortable as possible in their new surroundings to ensure they thrive. As well as following the steps opposite, here are some additional hints to promote the chances of happy plants and, so, a happy gardener:

- Always check the height and spread information on the plant's label. If a group of plants is planted too near to each other, they will soon crowd each other out.
- It is especially important that you continue to water any spring- or summer-planted specimens during their first growing season. By their second year, they will have established a good root system and should not need additional watering.
- Some perennials may need support to stop them flopping over. Use twiggy sticks or canes and string and push them into the ground before the plants are fully grown so their new growth hides any supports.

When you initially plant a group of perennial plants, ensure you leave plenty of room between each one. The border may look airy at first, but they will soon join together.

How to plant perennials and shrubs

1
Make sure the soil is well prepared. Remove any weeds using a digging fork and turn the soil over, incorporating plenty of organic matter such as garden compost. Give the plants a good soaking.

2
Position the plants in their pots where you think they should go. Stand back and look from different angles. Only when you are happy with your arrangement, is it time to get them planted.

3
Dig a hole wider and slightly deeper than the plant's container. As you dig the hole, pile the soil to one side.

4
Gently remove the plant from its pot and place it into the hole. If the planting hole is too deep or too shallow, remove the plant and adjust to the correct depth. Remember that most plants should be planted so they are at the same depth as they were in their pot.

5
Position the plant in the centre of the planting hole, then fill in the gaps around the sides of the plant with soil, firming it down gently to make sure the plant is supported all the way around.

6
Finally, give your new plants a really good watering. They will take a few weeks to get their roots down deeper, so remember to also water them during dry spells until they are established.

Planting trees

You can buy trees either in pots from a garden centre or bare-rooted from a more specialist supplier. If you buy a bare-rooted tree, you must plant it immediately upon arrival. Any tree is best planted between mid-autumn and mid-spring, but not in frosty weather nor in frozen soil as the roots are then likely to suffer frost damage.

If you are buying a tree from a garden centre, there are a few things that are worth remembering:

- Look for a sturdy, shapely tree with healthy looking leaves.
- Avoid any that have moss or weeds growing in their pots – they have been there too long.
- Don't worry if the tree looks small; small specimens establish more quickly than larger ones. In fact, large newly planted trees take so many years to establish that smaller trees planted at the same time will often overtake them in size.
- Remember that the trees you plant in your garden are going to grow! So choose one that's right for its space.

Trees for small gardens

Acer griseum (paperbark maple)
Amelanchier lamarckii (snowy mespilus)
Betula pendula 'Youngii' (weeping birch)
Cercis siliquastrum (Judas tree)
Cotoneaster frigidus 'Cornubia'
Malus x *robusta* 'Red Sentinel' (flowering crab apple)
Malus x *zumi* 'Golden Hornet' (flowering crab apple)
Prunus x *subhirtella* 'Autumnalis' (Higan cherry)
Sorbus vilmorinii (Vilmorin's rowan)
Sorbus 'Joseph Rock'

A young specimen of Robinia pseudoacacia *'Frisia'. It can eventually grow to a height of 10–15m (30–50ft), so carefully considear its position.*

How to plant a tree

1
Consider the correct position for your tree. Remember not to plant any trees too close to your or your neighbours' house or it may eventually block out light and damage the building's foundations and drains.

2
Use a spade to dig a hole that is twice as deep and wide as the pot your tree is in. Throw some organic matter into the bottom of the hole and also mix some with the soil you have dug out.

3
Check for the correct depth by placing the tree in its pot in the hole. The ground level around the planting hole should be the same as the level of the top of the tree's rootball.

4
Before planting the tree, drive a stake into the ground at an angle of 45 degrees. It is important to do this before planting the tree so the stake does not go through the rootball. The top of the stake must be next to the tree's stem and approximately 60cm (2ft) above ground level.

5
Carefully remove your tree from its pot and place in the planting hole. Refill the hole with the soil and compost mixture. Using a tree tie, secure the tree to the stake. Protect the tree with a tree guard if there are rabbits in your garden, and water well. A mulch of compost, leaf mould or bark around the tree will help to conserve moisture and keep weeds down.

KIM'S TIPS

> Water your tree often throughout its first growing season and check the tree tie regularly. Wind can loosen the tree tie and as the tree grows, its trunk expands too.
> Remove the stake and tie after about three years when the tree should be strong enough to support itself.

Laying turf

If your lawn is in poor condition, it is possible to improve it through feeding, watering and weeding. However, sometimes the best option is to replace it. Re-sowing a new lawn is cheap but takes a long time to get a good result and requires more effort. Laying a new lawn with turf is more expensive but gives an instant effect and can be used again much more quickly.

Buy the best-quality lawn turf that you can, and lay it the day it is delivered. You will then be rewarded with a lush green, weed-free lawn.

KIM'S TIPS

> Mow your lawn regularly: it helps to reduce weeds.
> Don't cut it too short, though, as this may encourage moss.
> Choose the correct mower for your size of lawn.

Preparation

Preparation is the most important job in laying a new lawn. First you need to clear the site:

- Remove the existing grass by stripping off the top 2.5cm (1in) of soil. If your lawn is small, this can be done by hand; for larger areas, hire a special turf-stripping machine from a machinery hire shop.
- Then dig over and rake out the whole area. Again, digging over a small area can be done by hand using a digging fork, but for larger areas, hire a Rotovator.
- Once it has been dug over, use a soil rake to start smoothing out and levelling the area. Remove stones as you go, and break down any lumps into a much finer soil.
- During this part of the job you can also fill in or level out any bumps or dips that you may have had before.
- Then either walk over the soil with your feet, taking small steps so your footsteps overlap, or go over it with a heavy roller. This is to compact the ground lightly so that there are no soft spots that may sink afterwards.
- After rolling, lightly rake the surface once again, checking that you have the surface level.

Buy turf that looks fresh and green with no yellow patches. Remember that turf is heavy, so it's worth getting it delivered and left as close as possible to where you are going to need it. It is important that you check the rolls of turf when they are delivered; if they are yellowing reject the delivery.

Work out how many square metres (yards) of turf you need and add ten per cent for wastage. Any leftover turf can be finely chopped up and added to the compost heap where it will rot down into a healthy crumbly loam.

How to lay a new lawn

1
Choose a long straight line as the starting point to lay the turf. A pathway edge is ideal, and if there is no edge to start from use a string line to work against.

2
Once the first row is down, tamp the surface gently with a scaffold plank. Then lay the scaffold plank on the first row to kneel on in order to lay the second row.

3
With the second row, stagger the turf so that no joins meet at the same place where the joins met on the previous row.

4
Continue in this way, using a knife and straight edge to cut the turf where necessary. Use the scaffold planks to walk over the turf. You should not step onto or put anything directly on the newly laid turf. Walking across planks in this way also saves having to roll the new lawn.

5
When you have finished, don't worry about cutting any edge exactly, this can be done in a couple of weeks when the grass has rooted into the soil below. The most important thing is to give the new lawn a good soaking, and continue to water it on any dry days.

Watering

Without sufficient water, plants just cannot grow. It must be the most important requirement of any plant. Of course, we can all tell that our hanging baskets need watering on a hot summer's day when we see the plants start to wilt, but what about the rest of the garden? And how can we adapt to the gradual change in climate that we appear to be experiencing?

I'm always buying new plants! In the summer months give all new plants a really good soak around the base after they've been planted. This is a more economical use of water than using a garden sprinkler.

At home in our hot, sunny garden, I have many drought-resistant plants that, given a warm, dry spell of weather, flourish and look brilliant. However, we do grow vegetables, tomatoes in pots for the kids, and I also like to plant up some seasonal flowering plants each year in various containers. These plants need plenty of water! I use water-retaining gel in containers, which I add to the compost before planting (for more information on this and other water retaining ideas in containers, see page 143).

During hot, dry weather do not rush to water everything in your garden. Most established plants will be fine without any additional watering. However, newly planted perennials, shrubs and trees, plants in containers and vegetables (which are themselves 90 per cent water) will need regular watering.

The golden rules of watering

- Give one good soak on a regular basis rather than a few light showers!
- Water the roots, not the plants.
- Water your garden in the cool of the evening as the plants are then less stressed by the sun and there will be less evaporation, too. By dawn they will have replenished themselves.

I use rainwater whenever possible, collected in a water butt and applied to the plants with a watering can. It's a therapeutic job for a warm summer's evening.

How to cut down your watering needs

You can reduce the amount of water needed in your garden by improving the soil's water-retentive properties.

Organic matter: Adding plenty of organic matter, such as garden compost or well-rotted manure to the soil, improves structure, helps to hold more moisture and provides extra nutrients for plants.

Mulching: You can also reduce water evaporation from the surface of the soil by mulching. Use a layer of organic mulch, such as leaf mould, bark chip or garden compost, to help keep in moisture. This works really well around shrub plantings and should be applied when the soil is already moist. It also has the added benefit of keeping down the weeds!

Apply mulches such as garden compost or bark chip from mid- to late spring. This allows the soil to warm up a bit while still being full of moisture. Always water the area before putting down a 5–7.5cm (2–3in) layer of the mulch of your choice. Pull organic mulches away from the trunks or stems of plants as moisture build-up can lead to rotting and damage the plant.

KIM'S TIP

> Rainwater is much better than tap water for all plants, so why not install a water butt? They are easy to fit to a downpipe of a garage, shed or greenhouse. Make sure that they are raised off the ground enough so a watering can will fit easily underneath the tap.
> Weeds require water and nutrients too. Don't let them compete with your plants – get them out.

Feeding organically

Just like us humans, plants need a balanced diet of nutrients to grow well. Without a balanced diet, plants just will not flourish, so we need to feed them according to their individual requirements and growing conditions. There are three main plant nutrients and they are commonly referred to as N, P and K.

An organic liquid fertilizer is a good way of feeding plants in containers; be sure to follow the manufacturer's instructions as overfeeding can harm the plants.

N, P and K

- N is nitrogen and is needed for leafy growth.
- P is phosphorus and is needed for root growth.
- K is potassium – or 'potash' – and is needed for successful flower and fruit production.

In addition, like us, plants also need much smaller quantities of other elements, which are found in most garden soils.

Avoiding chemical fertilizers

It is quite possible to give your plants all the nutrients they require without using chemical fertilizers. Most average garden soils already contain all the nutrients plants need. However, in a vegetable plot, for instance, constant demands are made on the soil for seasonal crop production. In these cases, it is important to replenish the soil fertility so that it does not become depleted of any nutrients.

The organic principle is to feed the soil's living creatures so that they can, in turn, improve soil fertility, which then leads to healthy plant growth. Using chemical fertilizers is quick and easy, and many people would say that their careful use does not do any great harm to the home garden environment. However, it is easy to 'over fertilize' using chemical fertilizers and also they do not add anything to the soil's structure. So for these reasons I prefer not to use them in my garden, using wholly organic fertilizers instead.

Well-rotted organic matter: This is a miracle substance! It is surprisingly satisfying to spend time in the garden in early spring pushing around wheelbarrows full of dark, well-rotted manure. Spread manure across your vegetable beds and it will add small amounts of the major nutrients N, P and K to the soil, as well as some minor nutrients. All this work means you will be rewarded by healthy, disease-resistant plants – and vegetables that taste just delicious.

Other organic fertilizers: Where plants have extra, individual requirements you can use are other organic fertilizers. Be sure to follow the guidelines carefully for use on the packet.

- Liquid organic tomato and vegetable fertilizer is an excellent feed for tomato plants as it contains a high level of potassium, but it can also be used for feeding all other flowers, fruit and vegetables. I find it particularly good on flowering bedding plants grown in containers.
- Dried blood is high in nitrogen.
- Bonemeal is high in phosphate.
- Rock potash is high in potassium.
- Pelleted chicken or farmyard manure and seaweed meal fertilizers are rich in minerals and other minor nutrients.

But above all don't forget the well-rotted organic matter! It does more than anything else to keep your soil healthy and your plants happy.

What a wonderful sight – a pile of well-rotted manure ready to be added to the raised beds in the kitchen garden. Make sure that yours has been left to rot down for six months to a year.

Pruning and training

Pruning is the cutting back of growth on a plant, usually using a pair of secateurs. It may be carried out to increase the floral display, to keep a shrub within its allotted space or to produce strong new growth. While I carefully prune my climbing roses every spring and coppice my willows to produce a good supply of stems for weaving, many of the shrubs in our garden just have the odd branch removed if it grows across a pathway or into another plant. If you never prune anything in your garden, your trees, shrubs and climbers will probably keep growing and appear to be quite happy. However, regular pruning is very beneficial as it maintains good health, encourages strong growth and helps to shape plants so that they look at their best. There is no big mystery about pruning, you just need to know why you are pruning a particular plant and how and when to do it.

This philadelphus clearly shows the current flowering growth and also the new, non-flowering shoots that will continue growing for the rest of the season and then produce flowers next year.

Shrubs to prune in late spring

Deciduous azaleas
Camellia
Clematis montana
Deutzia
Forsythia
Philadelphus (mock orange)
Ribes (flowering currant)
Syringa vulgaris (common lilac)
Weigela

One of the simplest pruning jobs in the garden is just to remove any dead, damaged or diseased branches. This tidies up plants and also allows a greater circulation of air around them. You can do this at any time, but usually spring is best as there may be some winter damage to remove.

You can help many flowering shrubs to produce a much better floral display by pruning to keep growth vigorous. How and when you prune for this reason will depend on whether the flowers are produced on last year's stems or on new growth produced this year. This sounds complicated but it is, in fact, quite straightforward.

Shrubs that flower in spring and early summer

These produce flowers on stems that grew last year. Forsythia, for example, produces its spring flowers on growth that it made the previous season. Therefore it should only be pruned immediately after it has flowered, and then left alone and not pruned for the rest of the growing season. Remove the stems that have just flowered by cutting them back to young side shoots. These will produce new branches that will flower in the following year. If you did prune it again in the autumn, you would be cutting off its spring flowers! This is the reason

Buddleja davidii is a shrub that flowers on the current season's growth and should be cut back hard each spring, otherwise it can quickly take over the garden.

why a trimmed forsythia hedge never produces as many flowers as a properly pruned shrub. If you don't remember to prune at the right time, just leave the shrub until the following year.

Shrubs that flower in mid- to late summer

These produce flowers on new stems that have grown during that season. Take, for example, a buddleia. In early spring it starts growing new shoots, which eventually flower in mid- to late summer. If the buddleia needs to be pruned, it is done in early spring. Cut it down hard and it will produce vigorous new growth and then flower from midsummer on.

Pruning to tidy up

Often plants may start to invade your living space within a garden. A different approach is required here as mature shrubs often provide privacy and good structure within a garden, so you'll probably need to sacrifice some flowers to keep the shrubs trimmed and in their place. If the plants are evergreen, the best time to give them a trim is late spring and preferably just after they have flowered. Use secateurs, not garden shears as they tend to rip and tear the leaves.

- Look at the overall shape of a mature shrub, and re-shape if necessary.
- Cut back any out-of-place or long, vigorous growths to leave a shape that is well balanced and pleasing to look at.

Sometimes a shrub may become too large and out of shape and quite often older shrubs become bare at the base and produce just a few flowers on the top. As long as it is not diseased, rather than pulling it out, it's worth trying to renovate it. This involves cutting down the whole shrub using long-handled pruners, or even a pruning saw, and leaving several woody stems only 50–75cm (20–30in) high. For evergreen shrubs, this is best done in late spring, but deciduous shrubs are best cut down during autumn or winter. Deciduous shrubs that flower on the current season's growth, such as fuchsia and buddleia, may be given this treatment in spring.

After cutting back, apply an organic granular fertilizer and a mulch to conserve moisture. Most overgrown shrubs cut down in this way will readily sprout into life again, producing a mass of healthy new growths. As the shrub re-grows, prune it as appropriate to create a bushy, well-shaped shrub.

Coppicing and pollarding

Some shrubs, such as golden-leaved elder (*Sambucus*), do flower but are mostly grown for their foliage effect. While these may be pruned back in spring to promote fresh new leafy growth, they may also be pruned in a different way for a very dramatic foliage effect. This method is called coppicing if done right down to ground level, or pollarding if a trunk or stem is left.

Coppicing is often seen on willows to produce an annual crop of long, thin stems that are then cut and used for basket making, and indeed for other willow weaving too. When carried out on ornamental garden shrubs, the results are amazing. For example, when the smoke bush (*Cotinus coggygria*) is coppiced, it produces masses of larger than usual leaves on long, straight stems. The leaves also tend to colour better and remain on the shrub later in the autumn.

Most dogwoods are grown for the bright winter colour of their red, yellow or orange stems, and these too are best coppiced, as young stems are of a much brighter colour than older ones.

To coppice a shrub: Use secateurs or long-handled pruners and cut the stems down to about 10cm (4in) from the base. Then apply an organic granular feed and mulch the plant well. This is best done in early spring before any sign of new growth. In subsequent years, cut back to 5cm (2in) above your previous year's cut. If you decide you don't want to continue coppicing a shrub, just leave it to grow naturally again.

Pruning climbing plants

Climbing plants include some of the most spectacular and beautiful flowering plants. They do, however, need attention to keep them growing against the support they are trained up. Left without attention they can become untidy and overgrown. The same principle of pruning shrubs also applies to climbing plants. So if your climber is grown for its flowers, you need to know if it produces its flowers on growth it has made the previous season or on the current season's growth.

Climbers that flower on new growth made during the growing season are pruned in the spring. These include honeysuckles (*Lonicera*), potato vines (*Solanum crispum*) and Chilean glory vine (*Eccremocarpus scaber*).

Below: *The smoke bush (*Cotinus coggygria*) does have attractive flowers, but if grown purely for a foliage effect, it may be coppiced each year by cutting it down hard in the spring.* **Bottom:** *The potato vine (*Solanum crispum* 'Glasnevin') flowers on the current season's growth, so to keep it tidy, it should only be pruned back in spring.*

Above: *Clematis have different pruning requirements according to the variety, so keep a record of which varieties you plant.* **Below:** *This* Schizophragma hydrangeoides *is a close relative to the climbing hydrangea. It is a self-clinging climber and needs little pruning.*

Climbers that flower on growth made during the previous growing season should be pruned, like shrubs, immediately after they have flowered. Using secateurs, prune out the stems that have flowered. You should be able to see lots of new leafy shoots on the plant when you do this – these are next year's flowering stems and need to be loosely tied in, horizontally where possible (see page 185).

Clematis: These are much-loved flowering climbers and quite rightly so as they produce the most fantastic flowers in a wide variety of colours, shapes and sizes. Different types of clematis flower throughout the year and for this reason they have different pruning requirements.

Many species of clematis, such as *Clematis montana*, generally don't need regular pruning. Most garden varieties have large blooms and all you need to know is when they flower. As a simple guide, most spring and early summer flowering clematis flower on the previous season's growth, and just need a light prune after flowering to tidy up the plant.

Clematis that flower in mid- to late summer are flowering on the current season's growth. These ones are best cut back hard in late winter each year, to the lowest buds on the plant. This will ensure a vigorous, bushy plant with a good floral display every year.

Self-clingers: Climbers use various means to support themselves, some have suckers and these are referred to as 'self-clinging' (for more information, see page 116). In general, these are grown usually for their foliage and include ivies (*Hedera*), Virginia creeper (*Parthenocissus quinquefolia*) and climbing hydrangea (*Hydrangea petiolaris*). The only pruning these self-clingers need is cutting back of growth when they start creeping somewhere they shouldn't.

KIM'S TIPS

> **Buy the best secateurs you can afford. They will be more comfortable to use and give you a cleaner cut. Higher-quality tools make any job much easier to tackle and tend to outlast their cheaper counterparts. Keep secateurs out of reach of children.**
> **If you accidentally prune off some growth that would have flowered, you won't kill the plant. It will still continue to grow and will flower again in due course.**
> **For alternate buds, make a pruning cut at an angle away from and just above an outward-facing bud. If the buds are opposite each other, cut straight just above a strong pair.**

How to prune and tie in climbing roses

Climbing roses will grow and flower quite happily without any training or pruning, but eventually all the flowers will be at the top of an untidy plant. Some simple pruning and training along horizontal wires each spring will give you more flowers on a neater plant. Roses blossom best off horizontal stems.

1
In spring, when growth has started, remove all growth that is less than pencil-thickness, such as old flowering growth. You will probably end up with many stems, so work with one at a time and tie each one into the horizontal wires.

2
Tie a length of garden twine to the wire with a double knot. It's important to use garden twine because as the rose grows, it will break the twine rather than getting strangled by it.

3
Loosely tie in the stem of the rose. Finish with a double knot again and trim any excess twine to keep it looking tidy. Do not be tempted to push any stems behind the wires; it will cause difficulties with pruning in the future.

The time to tackle a climbing rose is before growth starts in spring. If the rose is not too large, it is sometimes easier to untie all the growth and allow the climbing rose to fall onto the ground. This also gives you an opportunity to fix any extra horizontal wires that you may need to the wall or fence. Ideally, there should be galvanized horizontal wires from ground level upwards at 40–50cm (16–20in) spacings. When growth starts, flowering shoots will be produced along the whole length of the horizontal stems; if the stems were vertical, just a few flowering shoots would be produced at the top of the stem.

Training climbers and wall shrubs

Most climbers other than self-clingers need some sort of support in the form of a trellis, frame or wires. The method of training climbers is to try to create a framework of stems over the support that you are growing the plant up.

- Take healthy, long stems and tie them in loosely using garden twine.
- Tie the twine securely to the support and then tie the twine around the plant, just below a leaf joint.
- Try to tie in stems horizontally rather than vertically as stems that are tied in horizontally will go on to produce more flowering shoots.

Above: *As the name of this shrub suggests,* Fremontodendron californicum *is an evergreen shrub that originates from California. For this reason it's best grown against a warm, sunny wall. It produces its bright yellow flowers all summer and is best left unpruned. Just carefully tie in stems to horizontal wires, but wear gloves as its leaves can irritate sensitive skin.* **Right:** *The potato vine (*Solanum crispum *'Glasnevin') is a sprawling climber that needs to be tied into suitable supports as it grows.*

Propagating

Propagation is very simply multiplying plants into greater numbers. This means that you can turn one plant into many over just a few growing seasons, saving yourself a lot of money. While a few plants may be tricky to propagate, many are easy, and remember, too, that plants want to grow! Help them along a little and you will soon have plenty of healthy baby plants in your garden.

Plants for hardwood cuttings

Buddleja (butterfly bush)
Escallonia
Forsythia
Fuchsia 'Riccartonii'
Kerria japonica (Jew's mantle)
Ligustrum (privet)
Philadelphus (mock orange)
Ribes (flowering currant)
Rosa (rose)
Vitis vinifera (grape vine)

KIM'S TIP

> When buying perennials, look out in spring for larger plants that have already filled their pots, as you may be able to propagate several plants for the price of one. Before planting, see if you can divide them into two or three pieces.

> When you replant any of your newly propagated plants, remember to prepare the soil, digging in plenty of well-rotted manure or garden compost (see pages 30 and 178). Then water regularly until they are established.

> Always propagate more plants than you think you will need. A few may not grow, and if you have any surplus, you can give them to friends.

There are many methods of propagation, but in the easiest examples, no effort is involved – the plants do everything for you! Groundcover plants such as periwinkle (*Vinca minor* and *Vinca major*) spread quickly and root new plants themselves as they go. Valerian (*Centranthus ruber*) spreads by dropping its seeds all over the place, from which seedlings soon emerge. The butterfly bush (*Buddleja davidii*) also does this, and can provide you with many new shrubs for your garden. Take time to look around your garden to see what plants are multiplying already without your help.

Self-sown seedlings: If you find some 'self-sown' seedlings of plants that you wish to keep, label them so you can find them easily again, and then in the autumn either pot them up or move them direct to their final positions. If you are potting them up, carefully pot them into small to medium-sized pots using soil-based compost. Water them well and keep in a sheltered spot outside until you are ready to plant them.

Propagating with hardwood cuttings: Not all shrubs provide new seedlings as readily as the buddleia, but many may be successfully propagated by taking hardwood cuttings (see list, above left). These are cuttings that are taken off shrubs in the autumn, and put into the open ground where most will root over winter to grow the following year (see page 188).

Propagating through division: Perennial plants increase a little faster than shrubs, and the best way to propagate them is by division. In early spring, when your existing plants are sprouting, it's possible to easily divide them into several new plants – for guidance on the art of division, see page 189.

How to propagate a pelargonium

1
Propagate a pelargonium in the summer by first using secateurs to cut a growing shoot that is about 15cm (6in) long. Make the cut just under a leaf joint.

2
Remove any flowers or flower buds and also the lower leaves.

3
Fill some small pots with fresh peat-free all-purpose compost, then use a pencil to make a hole in the centre of the compost.

4
Carefully insert the prepared cutting into the hole and firm it in by gently tapping the pot on your work surface. Give the cuttings a light watering, and place them on a bright windowsill where they will root in a few weeks. Only water them again if they wilt. Pelargoniums are best if kept slightly dry.

How to take hardwood cuttings

In the autumn, when the leaves have only just started to fall, select the hardwood plant from which you wish to take cuttings. Remember that deciduous shrubs are generally easier to propagate in this way than evergreen ones.

1
Using secateurs, cut vigorous, straight stems where they are about the thickness of a pencil. They may be quite long, so trim off the thin ends to leave a cutting about 30cm (12in) long. It is important to keep them the right way up – an easy way to remember is to make a sloping cut at the bottom and a normal straight cut at the top.

2
Plant your cuttings in an open but sheltered spot, with good soil. With a spade, make a V-shaped furrow about 20cm (8in) deep. Put the cuttings in upright and the right way up and spaced 10–15cm (4–6in) apart. Carefully fill in the narrow trench, so that the cuttings are two-thirds in the soil and one third above.

3
In spring, you should see some leaves sprouting from many of your cuttings. You will need to keep them weed free, and in dry weather they will benefit from a watering. Your new plants will need to stay where they are for the first growing season and they will be ready to move to their final position when they drop their leaves in the autumn. Although your new shrubs will be small, they will quickly grow and you will have the satisfaction of knowing that you have grown them yourself – and they have cost you nothing!

How to divide perennial plants

1
Use a digging fork to dig up a perennial clump. Then see if you can gently pull apart the clump with your hands, each small new piece should have some roots and a few growing shoots.

2
If the clump is too thick to divide by hand, borrow a second digging fork and insert both forks back to back in the middle of the clump. Push the fork handles away from each other and the clump should divide.

3
Replant all the pieces into freshly prepared soil with the growing shoots just visible above the soil level. Water well and wait for them to grow! You will be amazed at how quickly you can increase your perennial plants in this way. By summer this hemerocallis has come into flower. Next spring you can divide the plant again, quickly increasing your stock.

Perennials for division

Alchemilla mollis (lady's mantle)
Astrantia major (masterwort)
Crocosmia
Geranium spp. (cranesbill)
Hemerocallis (day lily)
Hosta (plantain lily)
Iris 'Sibirica Alba'
Nepeta x *faassenii* (catmint)
Phlox paniculata
Sedum spectabile (ice plant)

KIM'S TIP

> Some plants have thick fleshy roots and the easiest way to tackle these is by cutting. Place the clump on firm ground and chop in half with a spade. Take each half and chop in half again. Depending on the size of your clump you can continue in this way until you have several smaller pieces, each of which should have some growing shoots.

Overwintering

We all get tempted by the wonderful plants on sale at our local garden centre and sometimes buy something that needs a little extra care. Many specimens are originally grown in warm Mediterranean nurseries and they are then brought here for sale, which means there are an ever-increasing number of tender plants available to buy.

Some of these plants, such as olive trees (*Olea europaea*), are not entirely hardy and unless you are lucky enough to live in a particularly mild part of the country, they will need some winter protection. Other plants, such as cannas, ginger lilies (*Hedychium*) and dahlias, are tender perennials and they cannot be relied on to come through the winter frosts, so they also need some extra winter care.

Although it may seem like a lot of extra work to go to, many of these plants are particularly showy, and some will add a real touch of the tropics to your garden. So protecting a few plants over the winter is worth the effort.

If your plants do get frosted, don't worry! Leave them alone until spring and watch for any new shoots, and then only cut out dead wood, leaving the fresh new shoots. I have seen tender shrubs that have been frosted in an unusually cold winter re-sprout from ground level, quickly becoming mature specimens again.

Cannas are frost-sensitive plants that you will need to protect in winter. If you live in a cold area, they will need to be cut down before winter and mulched heavily or dug up and kept in a frost-free place.

Melianthus major is frost sensitive too. It is best grown in a pot that you can move under glass in winter.

Protecting vulnerable plants

Transfer to a covered place: If you have tender plants that are in pots, move them into a cool greenhouse or conservatory. Water them only a little during the winter, as over-watering may lead to the roots rotting. Bedding geraniums (*Pelargonium*) and marguerites (*Argyranthemum*) will not stand any frost and are best dug up and potted, cut

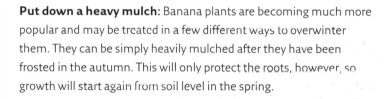

By growing frost-sensitive, or tender, plants you can create a completely different feel to a garden area. **Above:** This dramatic summer planting brings a touch of the tropics to a cool, temperate garden. **Below:** Tree ferns are best wrapped up for the winter, but not with plastic or polythene, which could encourage rot. Stuff the crown with straw first.

back by half and kept in a dry, cool and frost-free place. They really need some sunlight through the winter, so an unheated porch or a cool greenhouse is ideal. Water only a little to keep their roots dry and in the spring, when they start to grow again, start to water more often. Plant out when all risk of frost has passed. With bedding geraniums you can also take cuttings in mid-summer. These will root easily and can be kept on a windowsill indoors. They will take up far less room than if you dig up the whole plant.

Dig up and store: Herbaceous plants that form tubers, such as cannas, dahlias and ginger lilies, are best dug up at the end of the season, the top growth cut off with secateurs and then the tubers stored in dry potting compost until spring. These should be placed in a cool but frost-free place, such as a garage or shed. They should start growing again in the spring and can then be planted out when all danger of frost has passed.

Put down a heavy mulch: Banana plants are becoming much more popular and may be treated in a few different ways to overwinter them. They can be simply heavily mulched after they have been frosted in the autumn. This will only protect the roots, however, so growth will start again from soil level in the spring.

Wrap up the plant: Cut off the top leaves of a banana plant and wrap the whole plant stem in straw, held in place with chicken wire or Hessian. Alternatively, you can use several layers of fleece, which is a lightweight fabric that will allow light and water to pass through but help to retain warmth. It is available from any good gardening centre. The whole stem will then be protected from frost and growth will continue from the top of the plant in spring, which means you will get a much bigger and more impressive plant next season! Protect the tops of tree ferns by wrapping them in the same way.

Good positioning: Some plants that need a little shelter from frost are perfectly happy just by being correctly placed in the garden. Walk around your garden and identify the warm, sheltered spots and select these for plants that may be susceptible to a little frost damage. Avoid putting tender plants in obvious frost pockets or in exposed sites.

Growing edibles

Growing your own food is undoubtedly one of the most satisfying, enjoyable and immensely pleasing aspects of gardening. The feeling of pride you get when you pick your first vegetables, for instance, is immeasurable. The experience of sowing, caring and tending for the plants, harvesting a home grown crop and finally cooking for the table is something that you will never forget and it will continue to give you equal pleasure year after year.

KIM'S TIPS

> For crops such as salad leaves, beetroot and radishes it's a good idea to sow smaller batches of seed every two or three weeks. This will stagger the harvest of the crop, enabling you to enjoy it over a longer period of time.

> Visit your vegetables often and keep an eye on how everything is growing. By watching over your crops you can quickly deal with any pests or diseases that may appear on them.

Today a lot of people have concerns about chemical residues in shop-bought vegetables, herbs and fruit, and what effect this can have on our general health and wellbeing, and also that of our children. A great solution to this is growing your own produce. It's easy, fun and you know that your homegrown yields will be guaranteed free from harmful pesticides and other chemicals.

There is also the question of freshness. The taste experience of freshly picked vegetables is enormously improved from that of supermarket bought items, which, in many cases, may have travelled hundreds or thousands of miles between being harvested and being purchased by the consumer on the shop floor.

Vegetables

Do not think that growing good and successful vegetables is surrounded in mystery, you can do it quite easily and productively yourself. Do not be put off either by the enormous variety of vegetables that can be grown. In all cases I would suggest that you start with a number of well-known, everyday vegetables that can be grown easily. The exciting thing, however, is that you don't have to choose well-known, everyday varieties! A special variety of courgette or beetroot is just as easy to grow as the more common varieties.

The great thing about vegetables is that whatever size of garden you have, you will, if you want, be able to grow them. Even a patio garden can have vegetables growing in containers.

Opposite: *Some freshly harvested beetroot – not just the traditional red type but also pink and golden varieties that are just as easy to grow and still have the same beetroot flavour.* **Above:** *'Cavalo nero', or Tuscan black kale, is a delicious, easy-to-grow vegetable that also looks quite dramatic in the vegetable garden.*

KIM'S TIPS

> Apply organic matter to the vegetable plot in the autumn.
> If you wish, you can dig this into the soil when you apply it, but I find that an easier way is to spread the organic matter over the top of the soil and just leave it there. The winter weather and the worms will do much of the rest for you.
> A thorough forking over of the plot in the springtime will incorporate any remaining organic matter into the structure of the soil.

First steps: In any modest-sized garden, however, you should first choose the right spot for your vegetable patch. This is most important as a sheltered, open, but unexposed site will, without question, increase your opportunities for successful vegetable growing. The vegetable plot should be sunny to provide warmth and encourage growth and the ideal soil should be free draining but moisture retentive.

Don't be in too much of a rush to plant out your new vegetable plot if the soil conditions are not right. Time spent in making your soil more fertile, free draining and also moisture retentive will be time well spent. You will be rewarded with better crops, more admirable specimens and easier maintenance.

The digging in of well-rotted organic matter or your own garden compost will improve the structure of the soil and add to its nutritional balance. Not only will it make the soil more fertile, but your crops will be better too. However, your crops will use nutrients from the soil as they will continually require food. So it is necessary to replenish these nutrients and enhance the structure of the soil by an annual application of organic matter, such as well-rotted farmyard manure (see page 178), used mushroom compost or, of course, your very own garden compost (see pages 162–5).

Sowing your crops: Once the soil in your plot is suitable you can plan what you are going to grow. A common way of arranging vegetables in the plot is to simply form a series of long rows from the top of the plot to the bottom. You need access between each row on foot to sow, tend and harvest your crop. This should be the only area of the vegetable plot that you walk on. This is most important as the soil in the rows where the vegetables have been sown needs to remain moist, open and undisturbed.

• Laying something similar to scaffold planks between rows is a good and simple way to prevent damage to the adjacent vegetable rows.

• Another way of laying out your plot is to create a series of squares with pathways between. Each square would accommodate a single type of vegetable with easy access for all aspects of sowing, tending and harvesting. Consider building raised beds (see pages 94–7).

For summer crops, plant seeds outdoors when the soil starts warming up (see page 167). Sowing your vegetable seeds in rows will make it easier to recognize the weeds that will also sprout up, and it is important to keep the young vegetable seedlings weed-free as much as possible as they will compete for water and nutrients. Also, when your

vegetable plants start to grow a little more it will be time to thin them out. Just wash and eat the thinnings, these are the baby vegetables that supermarkets charge a premium price for!

Keep your crops well watered during dry weather. Vegetables are over 90 per cent water, and any lack of water will check their growth, and for some vegetables it may make them 'bolt', which is when they try to produce flowers and seed at the expense of the vegetable itself. If they start to do this, harvest them straight away.

After harvesting your crop: The ground will then need to be turned, any weeds removed and the soil replenished, ready for your next crop. It is best not to grow the same crop in the same place each year, as soil-living pests that are attracted to a particular plant can build up, and also specific nutrients can be depleted. The answer is crop rotation, and a simple plan of rotation is to grow root crops one year and above-ground crops the next.

Which vegetables?

Beetroot: Here is a vegetable with large, easy-to-handle seeds! Sow beetroot direct into the ground outdoors. Start to thin out the seedlings when they are about 10cm (4in) high – the leaves from the thinnings are your first salad leaf crop from your beetroot, and are delicious! Continue to pick more baby leaves as required. When the leaves are larger, they can be cut and cooked like spinach. Keep an eye on the developing root crop and harvest from ping pong ball size onwards.

I always sow some golden beetroot: 'Burpees Golden' tastes delicious and looks great in the vegetable garden. Other varieties to try include 'Chioggia', which has pink flesh with white stripes, 'Bulls Blood', which has very decorative red leaves and 'Boltardy', which is your standard red beetroot.

Courgettes: Sow the large seeds either indoors or directly outside where they are to grow. The variety 'Romanesco' is one of the best flavoured, while 'Tondo di Piacenza' has tasty round courgettes. Use courgettes cooked or raw in salads.

Dwarf French beans: Sow the large seeds either indoors or directly outside where they are to grow. French beans are an easy and trouble-free crop. We usually grow a purple-podded variety, 'Purple Queen'; they look great in the garden, and turn green when cooked!

Kohl rabi: An interesting looking vegetable, kohl rabi is a cabbage-type plant with a swollen stem. It is the stem that it is grown for, although the leaves are eaten too. Sow the seeds outdoors where they are to grow. Kohl rabi grows quickly and we grow a variety called 'Purple Vienna'. It has a flavour similar to turnips and is usually peeled, boiled and served tossed in butter.

Radishes: These are great for kids to grow as they are ready from sowing in as little as three to four weeks, make tasty snacks and are great in salads. They should be kept well watered; if not they may go hot and tough.

Runner beans: This really popular vegetable is decorative too – bright red flowers cover these climbing plants all summer. The main effort you need to go to with runner beans is to provide some support as they can climb up to 3m (10ft) high by the end of the season. Use bamboo canes or hazel sticks tied securely together, and simply plant the seeds at the bottom of each cane. When the beans start to appear, pick them regularly. If allowed to get too large, the beans become tough and the plants stop producing.

Salad leaves: In only four weeks after sowing you can be eating your own salad leaves. They are such a rewarding crop; the fine seeds are sown into rows in the soil and very quickly germinate. Look out for mixtures of different varieties – not just lettuces but oriental vegetables, chicories and herbs are included in some mixtures. The seedlings grow all mixed together and you pick off individual leaves, rather than uprooting the whole plant.

Shallots: Immature shallots are sold in garden centres during spring for planting out; these are called sets. Plant out these sets, which will grow quickly and produce about ten more shallots each. They will be ready in mid summer and they are great to use in cooking. We usually grow 'Dutch Red' or 'Dutch Yellow'.

Spring onions: Spring onions are easy to grow from seed and will eventually grow into large onions if left in the ground. We usually grow a purple-skinned variety for extra colour.

*Opposite (from top to bottom): Beetroot 'Burpees Golden', 'Boltardy' and the pink-and-white fleshed 'Chioggia' from Italy; courgette 'Romanesco'; dwarf French bean 'Purple Queen'. **This page (from top to bottom):** Runner bean 'Enorma', mixed salad leaves known as 'Mesclun'; spring onions 'North Holland Blood Red'.*

Herbs

I love to be able to gather fresh herbs straight from the garden to use in the kitchen. Many are easy to grow and some actually thrive in very ordinary soil. With the variety of shape and habit, flower and leaf colour, herbs make a real impact visually in the garden. I use some plants such as bronze fennel as an ornamental plant within my herbaceous borders, and I also grow a few plants in pots very close to the kitchen door so that I can quickly grab some while cooking. Many herbs also attract beneficial insects and pollinators, so whether planted among vegetables or on their own, they are a great addition to the garden.

Right: Perennial herbs are easy to grow and look great together in the garden. Below: Basil is best grown in pots in a greenhouse or in the warmest, sunniest place you can give it. Bottom: There are many types of mint, all with different flavours and all of them are easy to grow.

Some herb plants are grown from seed each year, some are perennials and some are shrubs. Generally, most herbs do best in an open sunny position and all are suitable for growing in pots. In fact, an arrangement of herbs in pots near your kitchen door looks great and is really practical. Herbs that are grown from seed I just sow in patches or rows among the vegetables.

Which herbs?

Basil: Basil is wonderfully aromatic and easy to grow but it does love heat and sunshine. For this reason I find it grows better in pots, started off indoors and then moved to a hot sunny sheltered spot outside (see page 193). Check the seed packets in your local garden centre and look for a packet of mixed basil varieties. There are about 20 different types of basil, from purple-leaved ones to lemon- or cinnamon-flavoured varieties.

Borage: The kids love helping me pick the bright blue star-shaped flowers from borage – great for edible decoration in summer drinks and salads. The borage leaves, though, have quite a crunch and taste of cucumber. Sow it once and it will self-seed in following years.

Coriander: A super flavour that's great in Thai cookery or try it added to any beetroot dish. Large seeds make it easy to handle and it likes

Flat-leaved parsley is sometimes called Italian or French parsley and is invaluable in the kitchen.

similar growing conditions to parsley, so does best sown in the warmth of mid-summer. If it runs to seed, harvest the seeds.

Dill: A great, quick-growing herb, we add it to new potatoes and it's tasty with fish too. Sow and forget! Likes reasonably good quality soil.

Mint: Easy to grow and great with new potatoes – young mint leaves are excellent raw in salads too. There are many varieties available, so smell before you buy!

Nasturtium: I'm never quite sure whether nasturtiums fit in as a herb or salad vegetable! Sow them one year and they will come up on their own in following seasons. They do best in poor, dry soil in sun, and I use the hot peppery leaves in salads and the large green, immature seeds in cooking – they are similar to capers.

Parsley: If there's one herb I can't be without, it's parsley. I prefer the flat leaf type, but cultivation is the same for this or the curly leaf variety. It's slow to germinate, so be patient and weed as soon as you can identify the parsley seedlings. It does best in a rich, moist soil. From a spring sowing it will usually last right through the winter, and then into next spring, when it will start to flower and then need to be pulled up.

Rosemary: This is a sun-loving evergreen shrub with attractive blue flowers in early summer and the leaves are particularly good with lamb. Plant a few bushes and only harvest a little off each plant.

Apples are easy to grow and one tree will provide you with a good crop every year.

Fruit

There is a wonderful choice of fruit that can be grown successfully by the amateur gardener. Many varieties have now been developed especially to make them more reliable plants that have a heavier yield of fruit and are more resistant to pests and diseases. Whatever you choose to grow, make sure the plants are suitable for the prevailing climate conditions in your particular area.

If you are fortunate to have a lot of ground, then you can create a separate fruit garden just as you would a vegetable garden. However, it is possible with many fruits that you can incorporate them into the general garden plantings, to good effect. As with everything else in gardening, preparing the ground is of the utmost importance. Digging over and nourishing the soil will help your fruits to establish more easily and to grow on more vigorously (see page 30).

*Gooseberries are easy to
grow and one plant will
reward you year after
year with delicious fruit.*

Which fruits?

There are so many fruits that you can, and undoubtedly will, grow
successfully but here are some of my favourites to get you buzzing
with enthusiasm. Don't be afraid to be bold and experiment, and
please don't be put off by failure.

Apples: An apple tree has a long life, so it will be with you for many
years. It is important then that you choose its location carefully before
planting. Ideally, it should be sheltered from the wind and open to the
sun. When choosing your tree, discuss with your garden centre all the
characteristics of the tree as they differ greatly in size, spread, fruiting
ability and flavour.

Before planting, prepare the soil well and then follow the steps on
page 173 for planting a tree. If you don't have much space available,
nowadays you can even grow an apple tree in a patio garden. A type
of apple tree has been developed that is generally referred to as a
'ballerina' type tree. This is because it is a single upright stem with
the leaves, flowers and fruits growing very close to the single stem.

Gooseberries: It is such a shame that this lovely fruit is not as
popular today as it used to be. I would recommend that you grow at
least one gooseberry bush. One word of warning is that you need to
handle the gooseberry bush with extreme care. The bush carries lots
of extremely sharp thorns, so always wear a pair of protective
gardening gloves when handling this plant.

The soil needs to be very well prepared as gooseberries will be
disappointing in poor soil. Once a young bush is planted, push
supporting canes into the ground up which you can tie the vigorous
new young branches that will carry the fruit. Gooseberries do not like
prolonged full summer sun, they do best in a cooler position. When
your gooseberry bush has become established, provide an annual
application of well-rotted manure around it.

Pears: If you can grow apples, you can grow pears. Everything I have
said above about apples is equally applicable to pears. So, again
choose the variety carefully, plant well and enjoy the produce!

Raspberries: Plant raspberry canes in the autumn. They like moisture
and a sheltered but sunny site. As ever, prepare the soil very well,
digging well-rotted manure into the area. Although this plant likes a
moisture-retentive soil, the planting site should drain freely.

There is nothing more exciting than watching fruit develop and grow through the summer. Raspberries need a little more attention than some other fruit, but they are certainly worth the effort.

To get the best from raspberries, plant the canes in a row at intervals of 40cm (16in) and to a depth of 5–10cm (2–4in). Then prune the canes back to a height of about 40cm (16in). Raspberries are best trained on wires, so knock in strong wooden posts at 2m (6ft) intervals along the length of the row and attach either wire or nylon string to these posts at three heights – 75cm (2ft), 1m (3ft) and 1.5m (4ft). The wires will help support the plant throughout its growth, providing you loosely tie the stems to the wires as they grow.

In the spring, apply a dressing of well-rotted manure along each side of the row and water regularly. By mid-summer all the new canes that have grown will be well established. Once you have harvested all the summer fruit you should cut back to ground level the canes from which you have taken the crop, leaving the new canes to give you next summer's crop.

Strawberries: Think of summer and you think of strawberries – I know I do!

Strawberries are easy to grow and are an extremely tasty and satisfying crop. You don't need a lot of space either, as strawberries can be grown in pots, specially designed barrels or tower containers, and even growbags.

When first planting strawberries, it is important that you buy healthy young plants. They tend to give their best for three years and then the plants need replacing, so don't be tempted to buy larger, older plants as they will probably have been growing in their pots for some time.

Plant new plants in late summer or early autumn to get a good crop the following summer. You should plant in rows no closer than 40cm (16in) apart. When the plants are growing and the first tiny fruits appear, you should apply a layer of straw around every plant and between rows. This is to prevent contact between the fruit and the soil as the fruits are easily damaged, which would then leave the plant open to pests and diseases. As an alternative to straw, most garden centres now sell 'strawberry mats'.

Strawberries need regular watering. Try to ensure that the bed does not dry out by maintaining an evenly moist soil throughout the growing season. Be careful, too, to keep strawberry beds free from weeds. They will compete with the fruit for nourishment from the soil and, in some cases, attract pests and diseases too.

The birds also like strawberries just as much as us so you will have to protect the plants. Most people simply knock some wooden pegs into the ground over which you can then drape fine mesh plastic netting.

Part 6
REFERENCE

To get the most out of your garden, some jobs are best done at certain times of the year, and I've found it handy to create my own calendar to remind me of what needs doing when in the garden. The recommended plant section that follows is there to help you make an informed decision when you're standing in a garden centre or nursery, faced with an endless choice of plants, which can be very overwhelming. I've chosen plants that are both my favourites and are easy to grow – a winning combination!

The gardener's calendar: spring

General maintenance

- Prepare for renewed grass cutting this spring by checking over the lawnmower; we take ours to a local garden centre for an overhaul.
- As the soil is starting to warm up, now is a good time to apply a mulch to help smother weeds and retain moisture in the soil. Apply a 5–10cm (2–4in) layer of organic matter such as garden compost, leaf mould or bark chip, avoiding touching any plant stems (see pages 162–5).

Trees, shrubs, perennials and climbers

- Finish planting bare-root trees and shrubs as early in spring as possible (see page 172).
- Plant hardy herbaceous plants and shrubs, but never in waterlogged soil or frosty conditions (see page 170).
- Clear away old foliage that has been protecting the crowns of plants as well as providing food and shelter for wildlife. If you didn't manage to divide your perennials in the autumn (see page 206), they can be divided now. This is an easy and cheap option for multiplying numbers (see page 189). Herbaceous plants also make great Easter presents for friends – healthier than a chocolate egg!
- Prune grey-leaved plants such as artemisia, santolina and lavender (*Lavandula*) annually to prevent them from becoming woody and leggy. Only do this when all danger of frost is past, and avoid cutting into old wood.
- Spring prune last year's summer-flowering shrubs such as butterfly bush (*Buddleja davidii*), caryopteris, perovskia, Jew's mantle (*Kerria*) and deciduous California lilac (*Ceanothus*). All of these flower on new growth and benefit from being cut down to within 30cm (12in) of the ground or to a main framework to stimulate flowering later in the summer (see page 181).
- Most plants benefit from having a good all-over haircut after flowering, especially dispensing with dead, damaged or diseased wood to encourage strong, compact growth and more flowers next year. Spring-flowering shrubs to prune after flowering include forsythia, lilac (*Syringa*), *Clematis montana* and the flowering currant (*Ribes*) (see page 180).
- Most roses can be pruned now, too. As in all pruning, cut out any dead, diseased or damaged wood and prune at a 45-degree angle to an outward-facing bud, removing about two-thirds of the top growth. Tie in all new growth, too (see page 184). Climbers can have the previous year's flowering growth cut back to two to three buds of the main stem. Roses that only flower once, such as ramblers, should be pruned immediately after flowering.

Annuals

- Sow hardy annuals where they are to flower (see page 166). But in cold areas, the weather can still be icy, so don't be tempted to sow seeds outside too early. Few seeds will germinate if the soil temperature is below 7°C (45°F).
- In late spring, summer bedding will be in abundance in garden centres, but do be wary of putting plants outside too soon.

Bulbs

- Just after snowdrops (*Galanthus*) have flowered is the best time to split up clumps of them, re-planting them immediately. Dividing them will encourage lots more to grow.
- Leave on all bulb foliage for at least six weeks before tidying up. The foliage is photosynthesizing, building up the bulbs' energy reserves for next year's flowers.

Containers

- In late spring, fill your containers and hanging baskets with bedding plants. Keep baskets well watered and allow the plants to settle and start to grow actively (about two weeks) before placing outside. Only do this after all threat of frost is past and choose a partly shaded site.
- Plant clematis in pots to enjoy on the patio. Choose large containers at least 30cm (12in) wide and as deep as possible. Use potting compost mixed with a controlled-release fertilizer. Plant so that the top of the root ball is 10–15cm (4–6in) below soil level and then mulch. Use a wigwam of canes for support, or make your own with willow withies or hazel.

Lawns

- Spring is a great time to lay new turf. Remove all the stones and weeds from the area, level and firm down by walking over the earth with your weight on your heels, before raking level again (see page 174).
- Lawns are in need of tender, loving care. As soon as the grass has begun to dry out, mow with the blades set at their highest setting. Drag out moss, dead grass and leaves with a rake before pricking all over with a garden fork. This will alleviate soil compaction, which impedes drainage, making it harder for air, water and fertilizer to penetrate grass roots. Fill any holes by brushing in a top dressing of fine sand, peat substitute and good garden loam (available from garden centres). Apply a 'feed-and-weed' product before rain is forecast (see page 178).

Water features

- Trim any dead plant growth on pond plants and divide any clumps that have become overcrowded. Check and reinstall pumps that have been taken out during winter.
- Algae absorbs nutrients from pond water and releases oxygen, which benefits the health of the pond. It is only when it becomes over abundant and starts to decay in the summer that it becomes a problem. So it's safe to leave algae alone in the spring.
- If last summer you noticed that you didn't have a good enough balance of plants, then now is the best time to plant more.

Vegetables and fruit

- Start sowing vegetables inside ready for hardening off when the weather gets better and before planting outside after the frosts (see page 170).
- Sow pumpkins and sunflowers with the children, ready for planting out after the frosts. Have them name their pots to encourage them and perhaps buy them a little watering can to water with. Only plant out when the threat of all frosts is well past.
- Plant strawberry and tomato plants in containers.

The gardener's calendar: summer

General maintenance

- Take a notebook and camera around the garden to remind you of which plants will need replacing or moving in the coming autumn.
- This is the time for *al fresco* dining. Give your patio area a good clear-up – clutter gives you indigestion! See if you need to have garden lighting fitted by a qualified electrician or settle for candlelight ... there are plenty of beautiful options to add subtle light; citronella candles will keep mosquitoes at bay. A small water garden in a container can add beauty as well as being a soothing focal point. Make sure there are a few scented climbers planted nearby to complete the atmosphere.
- Trim deciduous hedges such as hornbeam and beech in mid-summer after the main flush of growth has been made. Evergreen hedging, such as yew, box and holly, can be trimmed at the end of summer. Make sure there are no nests with fledgling birds and if not completely sure, leave until the autumn.
- Maintain a regular watering programme, especially for newly planted perennials, shrubs and trees (see page 176).

Trees, shrubs, perennials and climbers

- Camellia and rhododendron flower buds are formed in the summer so make sure plants are kept moist as drought will cause flower buds to drop next spring.
- Lift and divide bearded irises. Lift with a fork, shake the soil from the roots and cut the rhizomes with a sharp knife into individual pieces, discarding damaged material. Cut the leaves back to a fan about 15cm (6in) high before re-planting in rejuvenated soil. Plant 15–20cm (6–8in) apart, with the rhizomes covered with soil only about halfway up their sides, leaving the top completely clear of soil.
- Deadhead flowers that are finished or rotten to encourage more flowers. Plants allowed to produce seedpods will use all their energy for that instead of producing new flowers.

- Hydrangeas will be looking lovely towards summer's end. The pink and blue *Hydrangea hortensia* are those commonly sold. Whether they stay pink or blue depends on the pH of your soil (see page 28). Acid soils with lower pH levels will turn the plant blue, even if it is pink, and higher pH levels will keep it pink. If you have a pink hydrangea and want to turn it blue, water it with a powder form of aluminium sulphate, available from garden centres.
- Prune back wisteria to about six buds (approximately 15cm/6in) from the main stem.
- Keep a close eye on your roses for any diseases that need controlling (see page 159).
- Take pelargonium cuttings (see page 187).

Annuals

- Give your annual flowers twiggy sticks for extra support if required.
- Late sowings of night-scented stock will flower in as little as six weeks, so it's worth sowing some in pots for deliciously scented autumn flowers.

Bulbs

- Late summer is the time to plant autumn-flowering bulbs. *Crocus speciosus* is a good bulb for naturalizing in grass (see page 122), *Nerine bowdenii* and *Amaryllis belladonna* will both thrive at the base of a sunny wall. *Cyclamen hederifolium* will seed itself under deciduous shrubs.
- Plant daffodils (*Narcissus*) by the end of the summer as they come into root growth earlier than other spring bulbs (see page 206 for planting tips). Plant *Narcissus pseudonarcissus* (Lent lily) for naturalizing. Good daffodils for the border include *Narcissus* 'February Gold', which flowers in very early spring. *Narcissus* 'Tête-à-Tête' is a small, vigorous variety and *Narcissus* 'Cheerfulness' has sweetly scented, creamy yellow flowers in mid-spring.

Containers

- Six weeks after planting, start liquid -feeding containers and hanging baskets with a high-potash fertilizer (see page 178) to stimulate flowering when the compost has started to run out of nutrients.
- Check container plants regularly now that the weather is becoming warmer to see if they need watering. Take measures to slow down water loss by using water-retaining granules when planting (see page 143). These are particularly useful for hanging baskets, which are prone to drying out.

Lawns

- Mow lawns at least once a week, but raise the cutting height in prolonged dry weather. Only feed the lawn in moist weather when rain is forecast so the fertilizer will be washed into the soil. Consider using a 'feed-and-weed' mixture to help control moss and other lawn weeds.

Water features

- Small water features will lose a lot of water through evaporation, particularly on hot days. Check the level regularly to make sure the pump is still covered in water.
- Water plants grow vigorously in the summer. Thin out crowded water lily leaves and remove blanket weed by using a pronged stick to wind round and round it (see page 90).
- Keep small water gardens in containers topped up.

Vegetables and fruit

- Plant out all vegetables sown in the spring or sow seeds directly where they are to grow (see page 168).
- Take measures to scare birds and deter slugs, etc. (see page 158).
- Feed container strawberries and tomatoes planted in the spring with a high-potash feed (tomato food) once a week (see page 178). Remove strawberry runners, which will appear mid-summer, to encourage the plant to keep producing fruit.
- Sow Swiss or ruby chard for a late crop of succulent and extremely decorative leaves. Swiss chard 'Bright Lights' will provide the WOW factor with stunning foliage. Better still, chard is a 'pick and come again' leaf crop and can be left to over-winter to provide another crop the following spring.

The gardener's calendar: autumn

General maintenance

- Now is a great time for planting everything from next year's spring bedding to bulbs, perennials, shrubs and trees, especially evergreens (see pages 170 and 172). The earth is still warm from summer, damp from autumn rain and the air is cooler, so planting now gives them plenty of time to get established before next year's hot summer months. Transplant deciduous shrubs and trees after leaf fall, when they have become dormant.
- Put a good use to all those fallen autumn leaves by making leaf mould to use as a soil conditioner next autumn (see page 165).
- Don't be in too much of a hurry to tidy away stems and seed heads in the borders. Clear away anything that looks soggy, and don't put anything too woody or sickly or diseased on the compost heap. Leave seed heads and berries for wildlife as well as for providing interest in the winter. My favourite seed heads that last well into winter include *Phlomis russeliana*, coneflower (*Echinacea*), sea holly (*Eryngium*), stonecrop (*Sedum*) and many of the ornamental grasses.

Trees, shrubs, perennials and climbers

- Most perennials benefit from being divided every few years to keep them looking at their best. It is also an economic way to create new plants (see page 189).
- Move any evergreen or deciduous plants that need re-locating (don't forget those photographs or drawings you made in the summer).
- Take hardwood cuttings (see page 188).

Annuals

- Autumn is the time to plant spring bedding plants such as polyanthus (*Primula*), wallflowers (*Erysimum*), forget-me-nots (*Myosotis*) and sweet Williams (*Dianthus barbatus*), which can all withstand frost. You'll find them in your garden centre if you haven't already sown some for yourself at the end of summer.

Bulbs

- Plant bulbs for flowering next spring – garden centres will be brimming with them. The rule of thumb is that the bulb should be covered with roughly twice the depth of soil as the size of the bulb, but always read accompanying instructions. Unsuitable areas for bulbs include heavy shade, very dry soil or very moist soil, and areas prone to strong winds. If planting in containers, use a soil-based potting mix and add coarse sand or grit as well as some organic matter to improve drainage. Bulbs do not like cold, waterlogged soil.

Containers

- Clear containers of summer plants, adding the potting mix to the composter, and clean the pots well (see page 140). Replant with evergreen skimmias, variegated ivies (*Hedera helix*), winter pansies and bulbs, such as snowdrops and early narcissus, for a display to last right through winter and early spring. Ornamental cabbages make an eye-catching alternative planted with purple and cream winter pansies.

Lawns

- Scarify, aerate and top-dress lawns. Scarifying needs to be done vigorously with a spring-tined rake and it removes any accumulation of dead grass and moss.
- Aerating needs to be done especially in places where the grass has been compacted, perhaps where children play a lot or on a path. The simplest way is to use a garden fork and force it into the grass at 15cm (6in) intervals. If you have a large lawn, it is well worth hiring a rotary aerator for this job.
- Top-dressing mixture is sand, peat substitute and loam, which has been sieved and it fills the holes left by the rake. Ready-made top-dressing mixtures are available from garden centres. Again, if you have a large lawn, it is better to hire a spreader. For smaller areas, use a shovel to spread the dressing evenly over the grass and sweep it in with a stiff brush.
- If you decide to sow a new lawn instead of turfing one, then autumn is also a good time to sow a new lawn as it will then have enough time to have grown by the following summer. Prepare the ground well in advance of sowing seed (about two weeks), removing all perennial and annual weeds (see page 160). Level the soil with a rake using excess soil from the high spots to fill in any hollows. Firm the site well, either with the back of a rake or by treading over it evenly, before raking the soil to a fine texture, like crumble mix. Leave for about two weeks to allow any further weeds to appear and remove them with a rake or hoe.
- Choose a seed mix suitable for your needs (there are mixes especially suited for shady gardens as well as meadow mixes with wild flowers), and sow half the seed in one direction and half in the other for an even application (alternatively, use a seed spreader for larger areas). Rake over the surface to lightly cover the seed with the soil, and water with a fine spray so as not to dislodge the seeds. Take measures to keep the birds away, and expect seedlings to appear within two weeks.

Water features

- Protect ponds from falling leaves using netting. Leaves will decompose during the winter reducing oxygen levels, which will threaten the wellbeing of fish, frogs and other aquatic life.

Vegetables and fruit

- If growing vegetables, spread a thick layer of well-rotted manure over the growing area (see page 178). This will break down into the soil over winter ready for planting up next spring.
- If eating raspberries in the autumn appeals to you, then choose 'Autumn Bliss'. This accommodating plant fruits on the current season's canes and needs no support, unlike summer-fruiting raspberries (see page 198). I've allowed mine to take over a corner of our vegetable patch where it has formed a small thicket. The children love to hunt for them and the birds don't seem too interested in them until much later in the season. Plants are usually available from autumn onwards.

The gardener's calendar: winter

General maintenance

- Winter is a good time to have any hard landscaping done, such as fencing, patios, pergolas or decking. If you're not sure of your ability to do this, then don't hesitate to employ someone to do it for you. This will save time and money in the long run.
- Look after your local wildlife by maintaining a birdbath throughout the coldest months and providing food. Many plants provide edible fruits and seeds, which not only decorate the winter scene, but support wildlife through the winter.
- Living willow structures can be planted in the winter. Willow is tolerant of most soils and sold in bundles. They must be kept in water until they are planted to ensure they will root. Create living willow screens, dens and tunnels for children, arbours, arches or sculptures (see page 103).

Trees, shrubs, perennials and climbers

- Prune out any damaged, diseased or dead wood from deciduous plants. Apart from this being the best time to prune (while the plant is dormant), it is very difficult to do when the plant is in full leaf in the summer. Hard pruning promotes more vigorous growth than light pruning, so if you have a lopsided shrub, prune back the weaker side more than the stronger to stimulate it to catch up (see also page 181).
- Coppicing or cutting back willow (*Salix*) or dogwood (*Cornus*) shrubs in late winter results in a mass of coloured stems for the following winter's display.
- Bare-rooted roses arrive in winter and should be planted into their permanent position as soon as possible. Dig a hole large enough for the spread roots and deep enough for the budding union (the swelling at the base of the stem) to be 2.5cm (1in) below the soil surface. Add well-rotted organic matter and a sprinkling of bonemeal to the hole. After planting, reduce stems to 10–15cm (4–6in) to ensure the first flush of new shoots emerge from the base of the plant, making it sturdy. Roses like a moist soil, so mulch well after planting with organic matter, avoiding directly touching the stems.
- Hard prune clematis that flower in the summer by cutting back the whole plant to about 40cm (16in) above the ground. Cut back to just above a pair of plump buds. This includes the deep purple *Clematis* 'Jackmanii', the mauve-pink *Clematis* 'Comtesse de Bouchaud', the sky-blue *Clematis* 'Perle d'Azur', as well as the *Clematis viticella* cultivars. Early spring-flowering clematis such as *Clematis montana*, *Clematis alpina* and *Clematis macropetala* can be trimmed back after flowering if necessary.
- Prune wisteria, reducing shoots to 3.5cm (1½in) from the main stem. Wisteria is pruned twice a year, once in summer after flowering (see page 204), and again in winter to promote plenty of flowering buds.
- Overwinter any non-hardy plants you may have (see page 190).

Annuals

- Have a good read of the new seed catalogues and get your seed order in early. Remember to refer to any drawings or photographs that you took of your garden in the summer to see what worked well for you.

Bulbs

- Plan for spring colour now. Plant tulip and hyacinth bulbs at twice their depth together with a handful of grit to assist with drainage (see page 206 for planting advice).

Containers

- Heavy, prolonged frosts can freeze containers. Where possible, move pots under cover, close to the shelter and warmth of the house. Bubble wrap and Hessian can also be wrapped around vulnerable wind-swept containers that are too big to move. This will help protect the root balls inside the container.

Lawns

- Keep lawns free of any dead leaves that may blow over them in the winter.
- If it is frosty, avoid walking on your lawn – you will damage the grass.

Water features

- To prevent frost damage, drain off outdoor water supplies and empty small water features.
- Remove water pumps to prevent frost damage.

Vegetables and fruit

- Shallots, broad beans and garlic can be sown or planted in winter, as long as the soil is not frozen or waterlogged. Shallots are traditionally planted on the shortest day of the year and harvested on the longest. Plant them 15cm (6in) between sets and 30cm (12in) between rows. Garlic has a long growing season, about six months.
- Broad beans will need their growing tips pinched out once the first pods have set to deter blackfly. 'Aquadulce' is a good variety to choose.
- Winter is a good time to have a good tidy-up in the vegetable garden. In dry weather, the soil can be dug over and improved, ready for spring.
- A wet winter's day is the ideal opportunity to clear out the garden shed, re-organize it and dispose of any rubbish.

Kim's recommended plants

The following trees, shrubs (pages 212-13) and perennials (pages 214-16) are those that I am particularly fond of and have planted many times. They are all relatively easy to plant and maintain, and I know will give you just as much pleasure as they have given me over the years. Throughout the book I have also included lists of 'Top' plants for different circumstances, whether it be dry or damp conditions, suggestions of colourful perennials and bulbs to naturalize, or just great colour options. As these are also my recommended plants, on page 217 you will find an alphabetical list of each group.

Trees

NAME	DESCRIPTION	GROWING NOTES
Acer griseum (paperbark maple)	A deciduous tree that has deep green, three-lobed leaves. It has attractive peeling bark that is a rich mahogany brown colour. While its colourful bark provides winter interest, the paperbark maple is at its most stunning in autumn. Red and scarlet leaves look fantastic with the richly coloured bark. Grows up to 10m (30ft).	It is happy in an open position on most ordinary soils.
Amelanchier lamarckii (snowy mespilus)	A delightful deciduous tree with a light, airy feel to it. The pretty spring flowers are white and they appear as the new leaves are unfolding. The new leaves are a coppery colour and they gradually turn greener, until autumn when the tree puts on a stunning display of red, orange and yellow foliage. Usually grows to 4.5–6m (15–20ft).	You will find amelanchier in a garden centre being sold as a shrub and also as a tree. The ones sold as trees have just been grown into a tree shape before they are sold. If you plant one that is sold as a shrub you will still get a lovely plant, it will just be bushier and multi-stemmed, rather than single stemmed. Amelanchier prefers a moist, well-drained lime-free soil.
Betula pendula 'Youngii' (weeping birch)	A weeping form of the common silver birch. It is a small, dome-shaped, deciduous tree with bright green leaves and a silvery trunk. Its weeping habit is a good contrast for more upright shapes, and its leaves turn a lovely clear yellow in the autumn. Grows up to 8m (25ft).	Tolerant of all soils. The pendulous branches often come right down to the ground like curtains, and if it's planted on a lawn, it makes a leafy den for kids to play in!
Cercis siliquastrum (Judas tree)	This deciduous, small, bushy tree has masses of lovely pink flowers in mid-spring, followed by attractive heart-shaped leaves, which are bronze tinted when young, turning dark bluish-green during summer, then bright yellow in autumn. Grows up to 10m (30ft).	As the tree originated in the eastern Mediterranean it enjoys a sunny position and well-drained soil, although it is frost hardy. It is only usually sold as a small shrub, as it does not transplant well as a larger tree.

NAME	DESCRIPTION	GROWING NOTES

Cotoneaster

Cotoneaster frigidus 'Cornubia' is a vigorous semi-evergreen large shrub or small tree with spreading, arching branches. In most winters it remains evergreen but it loses its leaves during very cold weather, with new ones growing the following spring. It carries fragrant white flowers in early summer that are attractive to bees. These flowers are followed by clusters of showy, large red fruits that hang down and persist for many weeks – eventually birds will make a meal of them! Grows up to 6m (20ft).

Cotoneaster frigidus 'Cornubia' is happy in most soils, in an open position. Because of its spreading habit, it can take up a bit of space, but for its flowers, usually evergreen leaves and bright red berries, it is well worth the space.

Malus x robusta 'Red Sentinel' and Malus x zumi 'Golden Hornet' (crab apples)

Both of these flowering crab apples are real favourites of mine. I have both in my garden and although they are deciduous trees, they are a delight throughout the year. White spring flowers cover the branches and are pink in bud, just like the usual apple blossom. The leaves are fresh and green in summer, with golden tints in the autumn. These trees are, of course, grown for their fruit, and 'Golden Hornet' has masses of bright yellow fruits throughout the autumn. The variety 'Red Sentinel' has clusters of bright red, cherry-sized fruits that last all winter. Both varieties look particularly attractive after the leaves have fallen, with just the colourful fruits adorning the bare branches. Both varieties usually grow up to 4.5m (15ft).

Both do well in most soils, in an open sunny position.

Prunus x subhirtella 'Autumnalis' (Higan cherry)

A small deciduous tree with attractive green leaves in summer, which turn yellow and orange during autumn. Lovely small, white flowers are produced on the bare twigs and branches from late autumn right through to early spring. The winter-flowering cherry is a very welcome sight on a cold winter's day. There is also a pale pink flowered version called 'Rosea'. Grows up to 8m (25ft).

Likes to grow in a moist but well-drained soil.

Sorbus 'Joseph Rock' and Sorbus vilmorinii (rowan)

These two trees are small-growing, deciduous trees with graceful, fern-like foliage. Both varieties have heads of creamy white flowers, followed by large clusters of berries. *Sorbus vilmorinii* has berries that are rosy red at first, gradually turning white flushed with pink. Sorbus 'Joseph Rock' has creamy yellow berries that deepen in colour and remain on the tree well after the leaves have fallen. On both varieties, the green summer leaves turn amazing shades of red, orange, purple and yellow in the autumn. *Sorbus* 'Joseph Rock' grows up to 10m (30ft); *Sorbus vilmorinii* up to 5m (15ft).

Rowans are easy to grow in any open situation, and are a colourful addition to any garden.

Shrubs

NAME	DESCRIPTION	GROWING NOTES
Buddleja davidii	No garden should be without a butterfly bush! *Buddleja davidii* is fast growing, has attractive, highly scented flowers, and, of course, attracts many, many butterflies. Grows up to 3m (10ft).	Flowers on the growth that is made during the current season so cut it back hard in late spring, for a good mid-summer display. Do not deadhead the flowers: the seeds are a favourite winter food of many small birds.
Choisya ternata (Mexican orange blossom)	A wonderful evergreen shrub, it forms a dense rounded bush and has very shiny, dark green leaves. It has scented white flowers in late spring and usually again in the autumn. Grows up to 2.5m (8ft).	Useful for providing structure in the garden and it's tolerant of poor soil, shade and dryness once established. A really good evergreen shrub. Responds well to pruning.
Hydrangea quercifolia (oak-leaved hydrangea)	The oak-leaved hydrangea has large bold leaves, but also white flowers in mid- to late summer. This is classed as a deciduous shrub but it often hangs onto its leaves for most of the winter; the foliage usually colours red and purple during the autumn too. Grows up to 1m (3ft). 	Not fussy about soil but looks best in a slightly shaded position.
Philadelphus (mock orange)	This is a medium to large deciduous shrub. It is usually grown for its highly scented white flowers that appear in early summer and has fresh green leaves (there is also a golden leaved form). Recommended varieties are 'Belle Etoile', 'Virginal' and *Philadelphus microphyllus*. 'Belle Etoile' grows up to 2.5m (8ft); *P. microphyllus* up to 1m (3ft); 'Virginal' up to 3m (10ft).	A useful shrub as it grows in dry shade and is fast growing.
Phormium tenax (New Zealand Flax)	A fantastic evergreen, architectural plant. It would be an amazing contrast to *Viburnum plicatum* f. *tomentosum* 'Mariesii', or a similar plant with horizontal qualities. It looks great on its own and with contemporary architecture or accessories. It's also really good as a container plant. *Phormium tenax* has plain green leaves, and is the largest-growing phormium. However, there are many new phormium varieties available in a wide colour range and also with yellow, pink and purple variegated leaves. Grows up to 4m (12ft).	Some varieties are slightly frost tender, but if frosted they will usually sprout up again quickly. Some species are also not so tall-growing and are suitable for smaller spaces.

NAME	DESCRIPTION	GROWING NOTES
Potentilla fruticosa	A small-growing, bushy, deciduous shrub flowering from May to September – that's five months of flowering! The flowers are small and come in a wide colour range: white, cream, pale yellow, bright yellow, pink, red and orange. The shrub is generally a rounded shape, and it has bright green leaves. Grows up to 1m (3ft).	Does not have any architectural quality, so it's best used as a filler between more dominant shapes. It flowers on the current year's growth, so it can be cut back in early spring if required, without the loss of summer flowers.
Skimmia japonica 	Skimmias are dome-shaped, aromatic, evergreen shrubs and they have attractive scented flowers, which are followed by bright red berries. *Skimmia japonica* is available as either a male or female plant; only the female carries the berries but the male plant is equally beautiful. The most widely grown variety of the male form is called 'Rubella', which has lovely flowers that are red in bud, opening white. Grows up to 1m (3ft).	Tolerant of all types of soil. To make sure you get a good show of red berries on your female skimmias, you need a male plant for pollination. It doesn't need to be planted right next to the female; as long as it is not too far away, the bees will do their job.
Sorbaria sorbifolia	This is a rather handsome deciduous shrub. It has handsome feathery green leaves and in mid-summer it produces creamy white flowers. The flowers have a slightly weeping habit, and the leaves are particularly attractive. Grows up to 2m (6ft).	Happy in any type of soil, but best in an open position.
Viburnum tinus (laurustinus) 	A widely planted, medium-sized, evergreen shrub with dark green, shiny leaves. It has white flowers that open from late autumn to early spring. The flowers are pink in bud and are very attractive for many weeks before they open. Flowers are followed by bluish-black small berries. Grows up to 3m (10ft).	A very attractive winter shrub always looks cheerful, whatever time of year it is.
Viburnum plicatum f. *tomentosum* 'Mariesii' (Japanese snowball bush)	A large-growing deciduous shrub that has white flowers in early summer. It has a strong form to it with layers of horizontal branches; the flowers are born on top of these layers. Grows up to 2.5m (8ft).	I often plant this shrub on a corner where it can freely spread its magnificent branches.

Perennials

NAME	DESCRIPTION	RECOMMENDED VARIETIES	GROWING NOTES
Alchemilla mollis (lady's mantle) 	This is a vigorous, clump-forming perennial. It has apple-green leaves that drops of water almost dance on so it, of course, looks particularly good after rain! The flowers are a frothy mass of tiny, tiny individual lime-green flowers; there is only one main flush of flowers but they last for many weeks. Grows up to 60cm (24in).	There is only one variety – just ask for *Alchemilla mollis* or lady's mantle.	Make good cut flowers, lasting well in water and usefully filling all the gaps between other cut flowers. When the main flush of flowers starts to brown I like to cut all the plant's growth down to ground level with a pair of shears; fresh new foliage and just a few more flowers quickly appear.
Anemone hupehensis var. *japonica* (Japanese anemone)	Japanese anemones, or windflowers, flower from late summer to mid-autumn. They are tall plants with very simple fresh-looking flowers in white or pink. Once established they spread themselves without any extra help!	*Anemone hupehensis* 'Prinz Heinrich': semi-double dark pink flowers. Grows up to 90cm (36in). *Anemone hupehensis* 'September Charm': single pale pink flowers. Grows up to 90–120cm (36–48in). *Anemone* x *hybrida* 'Honorine Jobert': white single flowers on tall plants. Grows up to 120–140cm (48–56in).	Grow happily in dry shade. The white-flowered varieties look especially good in shade, and they are equally at home in borders or in semi-wild areas.
Astrantia (Hattie's pincushion) 	Astrantias are not the showiest or most flamboyant of flowers but they do have a lovely quality all of their own. They attract bees and butterflies, and can flower continuously from late spring to mid-autumn if deadheaded. Make sure you take a close look at the astrantia flowers as they are quite beautiful. They make excellent, long-lasting cut flowers.	*Astrantia* 'Hadspen Blood': dark crimson flowers, with lovely wine-red-tinted foliage. Grows up to 80cm (32in). *Astrantia major* subsp. *involucrata* 'Shaggy': white and green flowers on vigorous plants. Grows up to 80cm (32in). *Astrantia maxima*: lovely soft pink and pale green flowers, a little later than the other two here to start flowering, but worth the wait. Grows up to 70cm (28in).	Do well in any reasonable garden soil but do appreciate a moisture-retentive soil, given a moist spot they also do well in part shade. They are easy to propagate by division.

NAME	DESCRIPTION	RECOMMENDED VARIETIES	GROWING NOTES
Crocosmia	With yellow, red or orange flowers and sword-like foliage, these plants give a splash of late summer and autumn colour.	*Crocosmia* 'Lucifer': It has brilliant red flowers, carried above tropical-looking leaves, in mid-summer. Grows up to 1.2m (4ft).	Happy in sun or shade, and usually needs no help to spread! A strongly architectural plant that looks good in a mixed border, or use it in a tropical planting scheme.
Echinops (globe thistles)	The globe thistles produce steely blue, globular heads of flowers that for many weeks are highly decorative, even when they are only in bud. When each tiny flower in the globe begins to open bees and butterflies find them irresistible! Globe thistles are highly ornamental; they are tall upright perennials with silvery foliage.	*Echinops ritro* 'Veitch's Blue': small, steel-blue, ball-shaped flowers from mid- to late summer; grows up to 1.5m (5ft). *Echinops sphaerocephalus* 'Niveus': seeds itself around prolifically and its sturdy, globular flower heads have a white bloom. A plant best placed where it has room to spread itself about. Grows up to 2m (6ft).	Drought-resistant and contrast well with ornamental grasses such as *Stipa gigantea*.
Geranium 	Perennial geraniums should not to be confused with those bright red bedding plants, which are really pelargoniums. In fact, geraniums come in a range of colours, mostly pinks, purples, blues and white. They have a long flowering season, are very popular with bees and their soft colours mix harmoniously with other perennials.	*Geranium sanguineum* var. *striatum*: a low-growing variety with saucer-shaped shell pink flowers with darker veins. Very long-flowering and suitable for between paving or at the edge of a path. Grows up to 10cm (4in). *Geranium* 'Johnson's Blue': lovely, pure blue flowers on a spreading plant. It often creeps in and out of neighbouring plants, still producing its blue flowers. Grows up to 40cm (16in). *Geranium psilostemon*: this is the giant of the family. It has magenta flowers with a dark eye, it flowers for weeks on end during the summer, and its foliage takes on autumn tones at the end of the season. Grows up to 1m (3ft).	All geraniums are easy to grow and quick to give results. They are also easy to propagate by division (see page 189). Grow them in sun or part shade, and I find they also self-seed a lot, producing little baby plants all around the garden.

Perennials (continued)

NAME	DESCRIPTION	RECOMMENDED VARIETIES	GROWING NOTES
Hemerocallis (day lilies) 	Hemerocallis have, as their common name suggests, showy, lily-like flowers. Each one only lasts a day or two but there is a constant supply of them developing. Hemerocallis have attractive lush foliage, and are available in a wide range of colours. There are hundreds of varieties! So go to a specialist if you want the biggest choice of colours.	'Catherine Woodbery': large, scented, pale lavender-pink blooms. Grows up to 100cm (39in). 'Michele Coe': large, scented, very exotic-looking, peach-coloured blooms with a tangerine throat. Grows up to 100cm (39in). 'Pardon Me': small, bright red flowers; flowers for a very long period. Grows up to 75cm (30in). 'Joan Senior': creamy white flowers, ideal for a cool colour scheme. Grows up to 75cm (30in).	Grow well in most types of soil, in sun or part shade. They are quick to grow and easily divided in spring, to increase them.
Hosta sieboldiana	Hostas are grown for their bold foliage and do well in light, dappled shade. Container-grown hostas will need a soil-based compost and Vaseline spread around the rim to deter slugs.	If you are going to grow only one hosta, this is the variety you must grow! *Hosta sieboldiana* is a vigorous, large-leaved hosta that quickly forms a decent-sized clump. Its foliage is bold and steely blue in colour; which is a great contrast to grassy leaved and more upright plants. Grows up to 1m (3ft).	Easy to propagate by division and, most importantly, slug resistant! That means there is no temptation to use poisonous pellets. Also appreciates good soil but will tolerate dry shade.
Nepeta (catmint)	Nepeta does not just please cats but it is also irresistible to bees. My plants are buzzing with them all summer!	*Nepeta* 'Six Hills Giant'. It has pleasantly scented, grey-green leaves and produces spikes of small, soft blue flowers constantly from late spring to mid-autumn. Grows up to 75cm (30in).	At the end of the autumn use garden shears to cut down to ground level. Underplant with white or pale pink tulips, which will be set off by the emerging grey foliage. Prefers a sunny position.
Sedum 	Sedums have something to offer all year round. Attractive grey-green foliage in spring is followed by flower heads, which after being in bud for weeks, eventually produce pink flowers that attract masses of bees and butterflies. The dead heads turn brown, and look great in winter with the frost on.	*Sedum spectabile* 'Brilliant' and *Sedum* 'Herbstfreude'. Both have pink flowers and both grow up to 30cm (12in).	These dead stems need to be cut off in spring as the new growth starts. Sedums are neat upright plants, suitable for a sunny spot at the front of the border.

For more recommended plants, see these lists:

Glossary

Annual A plant that completes its lifecycle from seed to a flowering plant in a single growing season and then dies.

Architectural plants Plants that have a very strong form and create a bold impact whenever they are used in a garden.

Bare root Plants that are not supplied growing in a container. They have usually been grown in open ground and are dug up with little or no soil clinging to their roots.

Biennial A plant that completes its lifecycle in two growing seasons and then dies. A biennial usually grows leaves in the first season and flowers in the next season.

Bulb Usually an underground swollen stem from which a plant grows. Many bulbs die down completely during a dormant season.

Butyl rubber A strong rubber sheet used for lining water features.

Chippings Stone crushed into tiny pieces, which are used for surfacing. *See also* gravel.

Chlorophyll A substance in leaves that plants use to photosynthesize.

Climber A plant that climbs; in the wild they would use other shrubs or trees for support. Climbers may be perennials, annuals or have permanent woody stems – like shrubs. They may climb in a variety of ways, such as having twining stems, tendrils or tiny pads or roots that grip to a surface.

Compost Organic matter made from plant material that has rotted down and is used in the garden mainly to enrich the soil. *See also* potting compost.

Conifer Evergreen or deciduous trees or shrubs that bear cones rather than flowers for reproduction.

Coppicing The regular cutting back of shrubs, almost to ground level, to produce young, vigorous shoots .

Deciduous Plants that drop their leaves in the autumn and grow them again in the spring.

Evergreen Plants that keep their leaves throughout the year.

Fertilizer Available as chemical and organic matter and liquid to add nutrients to the ground. I prefer to use organic fertilizers (see page 178).

Focal point An object in the garden used to draw the eye in a particular direction. A container, an architectural plant or a piece of sculpture may be used as a focal point.

Garden centre A business that sells trees, shrubs and other plants, and almost everything else that is required in the garden. *See also* nursery.

Garden rooms A distinct space within the garden, which is usually partially enclosed. Garden rooms help to create more interest in the garden by dividing the whole garden space into smaller units.

Gravel Tiny stones used for surfaces. They are usually smooth as they have been dredged, as opposed to chippings, which are more angular.

Groundcover plants Plants that rapidly spread to form a thick, weed-suppressing carpet.

Half-hardy or tender Plants that will not survive a typical winter unless given special protection.

Hard landscaping The use of hard materials like stone or brick to create structures such as patios, pathways and walls within a garden.

Hardy The ability of a plant to withstand frost – hardy plants will survive a typical winter.

HDRA The Henry Doubleday Research Association. An organization in Britain that researches and promotes all aspects of organic gardening. Now also known as Garden Organic.

Hedge A line of shrubs planted to provide a screen, shelter or privacy.

Herb Herbs are generally edible plants that are used in cookery. They may be shrubs, perennials or annuals.

Leaf mould Organic matter made from decomposed autumn leaves and used as a soil improver or as a mulch.

Mulch A layer of material spread over the soil surface to help conserve moisture and suppress weeds. Can be organic (e.g. leaf mould) or inorganic (e.g. plastic).

Nursery A business that concentrates more on selling plants, rather than supplying everything for the garden. Nurseries often have a greater range of plants than a garden centre and may specialize in a particular group of plants, such as roses or perennials.

Organic gardening The principal of gardening without the use of synthetic or chemical materials, such as weedkillers.

Organic matter Materials such as compost, manure or leaf mould, derived from plants.

Peat A material usually formed in bogs and wetlands. While it is completely natural and organic, it is not taken from a renewable source so its use should be avoided.

Peat substitute A material that replaces peat in many potting composts and is taken from renewable sources. The most common peat substitute is coir, from coconut palms.

Perennial (sometimes called herbaceous perennial) A plant that continues to grow and spread from year to year. The spring and summer growth often dies back to ground level in the winter.

Photosynthesis The process in which plants produce food for themselves using sunlight, carbon dioxide, water and chlorophyll.

Pollination The fertilization of the reproductive parts of a flower. Pollen is usually transferred from one flower to another by insects, wind or animals.

Potting compost A mixture usually of sterilized screened soil, peat or peat substitute with added sand or grit for drainage and nutrients. It is used to fill pots and containers for planting up.

Propagation The production of new plants, which may be by division, taking cuttings or sowing seeds (see pages 186–9).

Raised bed A raised area in which vegetables are often grown. There are several advantages to using this method of cultivation (see pages 94–7).

Rotovator A piece of powered digging machinery, usually having a petrol engine.

Self-seeding Garden plants that readily disperse their own seed, which in turn then produce new plants.

Shrub Shrubs can be either evergreen or deciduous. They live for many years and the new growth they make each year becomes woody, building up a permanent framework of branches and stems.

Soft landscaping The landscaping of garden areas using plants, soil and grass. *See also* hard landscaping.

Statuary Garden sculpture.

Subsoil The soil layer beneath topsoil. It is poor quality as it is usually devoid of organic matter.

Tender *See* half-hardy.

Topiary Shrubs or trees that are fashioned into particular shapes by regular trimming. Most often created from box (*Buxus*).

Topsoil The fertile layer of surface soil (see page 28).

Tree A woody perennial plant that lives for many years and normally produces a single trunk and a head of woody branches. Trees may be evergreen or deciduous.

Vista A view that is often deliberately created within a garden for design effect.

Weed A plant that grows where it's not wanted. They are usually wild plants but some self-seeding garden plants may also become weeds.

Index

Author's acknowledgments

Special thanks to:

Nick Boyles
Emma Callery
Capel Manor Horticultural College
Barbara Clift
John Donnelly
Eastwick Plant Centre
Nikki English
Hal Fowler
Garden Organic (formerly HDRA)

Tudor Griffiths Builders Merchants
Ray Hale
Glyn Jones and Hidcote Manor Garden
Angela Newton
Rolawn Ltd
  www.rolawn.co.uk; tel. 01904 608 661
The Royal Horticultural Society
Bob Vickers
Wyevale Garden Centres plc

I would especially like to thank Richard Lucas. Richard and I have worked together for four years and were introduced when I was asked to design and build a show garden at the Holker Hall Garden Festival in Cumbria. We quickly discovered that we shared a passion for gardening, design and plants and have worked on several projects since. We were responsible for the planting design of the 'Enchanted' garden at Hampton Court 2004, which won an RHS silver medal. In 2005, we were delighted to win an RHS gold medal as well as Best in Category and the BBC People's Choice award at the Chelsea Flower Show with our own design 'The Cumbrian Fellside Garden'. Richard is an inspired and gifted plantsman and designer and it has been wonderful working with and learning from him. Long may it continue.